Cajun Cookbook

Cajun Recipes from the Heart of America's Deep South

By
BookSumo Press

Published by:
http://www.booksumo.com

LEGAL NOTES

Table of Contents

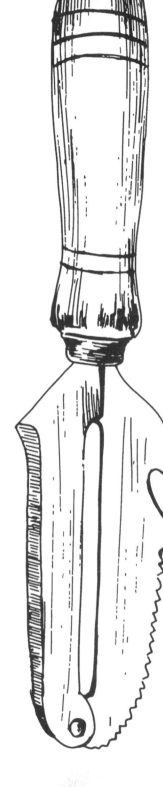

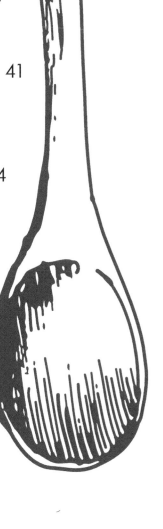

Southern Lunch Box: (Spicy Corn Salad) 53

Creole Seafood Fillets 54

Creole Alfredo 55

Creole Rump Rolls 56

Lemon Creole Chicken 57

Homemade Spicy Mustard 58

Creole Pizza 59

Creole Shrimp Tortillas 60

Creole Ice Cream 61

Cajun Sausage Kabobs 62

Creole Shrimp Bites 63

Creole Fried Crabs 64

Spicy Ginger Cake 65

Herbed Chicken and Cajun Skillet 66

Mild Cajun Eggplant Casserole 67

Creole Any-Noodles Salad 68

White Fish and Creole Potato Casserole 69

Okra Jumbo Stew 70

Smoked Venison Jerky 71

Rice and Beans 72

Easy Chicken Fry 73

Etouffee 74

Shrimp Bake 75

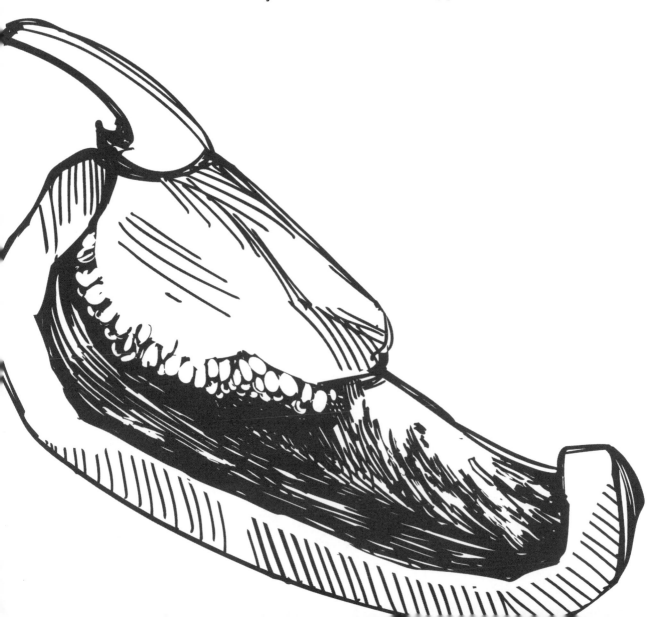

Cajun
Chicken Cutlets

🥣 Prep Time: 10 mins
🕐 Total Time: 55 mins

Servings per Recipe: 6
Calories	402.4
Fat	22.0g
Cholesterol	117.1mg
Sodium	659.7mg
Carbohydrates	16.1g
Protein	32.9g

Ingredients

3/4 C. rice flour
2 tbsp Cajun seasoning, blend.
1/4 C. butter
1 (2 lb) bags chicken breasts, strips

1/2 C. hot pepper sauce

Directions

1. Before you do anything, preheat the oven to 400 F.
2. Get a large mixing bowl: Mix in it the Cajun seasoning with flour, a pinch of salt and pepper.
3. Coat the chicken strips with the hot sauce then dust them with the flour mix.
4. Place the chicken strips on a lined up baking sheet. Cook them in the oven for 46 min.
5. Place a large pan over medium heat.
6. Enjoy.

BLACKENED
Lobster Sauce

Prep Time: 15 mins

Total Time: 30 mins

Servings per Recipe: 6
Calories	122.2
Fat	6.1g
Cholesterol	112.4mg
Sodium	435.9mg
Carbohydrates	2.7g
Protein	13.7g

Ingredients

3 slices turkey bacon
3 garlic cloves, chopped
1 bell pepper, diced
3 green onions, diced
3/4 C. broth
1 tsp Cajun spice
1 tsp Old Bay Seasoning
1/2 tsp onion powder
1/2 tsp garlic powder

1/2 tsp lemon pepper
1/2 tsp oregano
1 lb lobster
1/8 tsp pepper
1/4 C. heavy cream
salt

Directions

1. Place a large pan over medium heat. Cook in the bacon until it become crisp. Drain it and place it aside.

2. Keep 1 tbsp of bacon fat in the pan and discard the remaining fat. Cook in it the pepper with garlic for 3 min.

3. Stir in the onion and cook them for 3 min. Slice the cooked bacon into bite size pieces then stir it into the pan with the broth.

4. Stir in the Cajun, old bay, onion powder, garlic powder, lemon pepper, oregano, and pepper.

5. Cook them for 2 min. Stir in the lobster and cook them for 4 min. Fold the cream into the sauce then heat it for 2 min.

6. Serve your lobster sauce with some pasta.

7. Enjoy.

How to Make
Catfish

Prep Time: 30 mins
Total Time: 50 mins

Servings per Recipe: 6
Calories	195.9
Fat	15.1g
Cholesterol	36.9mg
Sodium	74.0mg
Carbohydrates	1.9g
Protein	13.1g

Ingredients
1 lb catfish fillet
1 tbsp lemon juice
2 tbsp olive oil
1 tbsp Cajun seasoning
1 tsp thyme
1/3 C. pecans, chopped
2 tbsp parmesan cheese, grated

1 tbsp dry breadcrumbs
1 tbsp parsley, chopped

Directions
1. Before you do anything, preheat the oven to 425 F.
2. Get a large mixing bowl: Mix in it the oil, Cajun seasoning, lemon juice and thyme.
3. Coat the fish fillets with half of the seasoning mix.
4. Get a mixing bowl: Mix in it the breadcrumbs, chopped pecans, parsley, parmesan cheese and the remaining half of the oil mixture.
5. Press the mixture into the fish fillets and place them on a lined up baking sheet.
6. Cook them in the oven for 7 min. Flip them and cook them for an extra 7 min. Serve your fish fillets warm.
7. Enjoy.

POT PIE
Creole

Prep Time: 1 hr
Total Time: 1 hr 40 mins

Servings per Recipe: 6
Calories	438.6
Fat	25.2g
Cholesterol	92.2mg
Sodium	500.0mg
Carbohydrates	34.6g
Protein	19.2g

Ingredients

1 pie crust dough
2 large cooked chicken breasts, chopped
2 C. frozen mixed vegetables
3/4 C. chopped potato, diced
1/4 C. butter
1/3 C. all-purpose flour
1 1/2 C. chicken broth
1 C. milk

1 tbsp Cajun seasoning
salt and pepper
1 egg, beaten

Directions

1. Before you do anything, preheat the oven to 400 F.
2. Place a pot over medium heat. Mix in it the flour, Cajun seasoning, salt, and pepper.
3. Mix into it the milk with broth. Cook them until they start boiling while stirring it all the time.
4. Fold the chicken, mixed vegetable, and potatoes into the batter.
5. Pour the mix into a greased baking glass dish.
6. Roll the pie crust on a slightly floured surface then drop it over the filling and cut off the edges.
7. Coat the crust with the beaten egg then place it in the oven and let it cook for 38 min. serve your pie warm.
8. Enjoy.

Tulane
Dorm Dinner

🥄 Prep Time: 25 mins
🕐 Total Time: 50 mins

Servings per Recipe: 5
Calories	409.1
Fat	20.2g
Cholesterol	102.1mg
Sodium	1026.7mg
Carbohydrates	28.4g
Protein	27.4g

Ingredients

1 lb lean ground turkey
1 small red bell pepper, chopped
2 tsp Cajun seasoning
2 C. hot water
1 C. milk

1 boxes Hamburger Helper cheeseburger macaroni
1 C. shredded Monterey jack pepper cheese

Directions

1. Place a large pan over medium heat. Brown in it the turkey, bell pepper and Cajun seasoning for 8 min.
2. Drain and discard the excess grease. Stir in the hot water, milk and uncooked pasta and sauce mix. Cook them until they start boiling.
3. Lower the heat and put on the lid. Cook the sauce for 14 min. Stir in the cheese until it melts. Serve it hot.
4. Enjoy.

CREOLE
Vegetarian Casserole

Prep Time: 15 mins

Total Time: 20 mins

Servings per Recipe: 4
Calories	173.4
Fat	3.5g
Cholesterol	57.1mg
Sodium	332.9mg
Carbohydrates	30.2g
Protein	8.0g

Ingredients

1/2 tsp salt
3/4 tsp sweet paprika
1/4-1/2 tsp cayenne pepper, to taste
1/2 tsp ground black pepper
1/4 tsp dried thyme leaves
1 1/2 lbs summer squash or 1 1/2 lbs zucchini, cut in rounds
1/2 C. whole wheat flour

1/2 C. cornmeal
1/2 C. milk
1 egg
safflower oil

Directions

1. Get a mixing bowl: Mix in it the salt, spices, and thyme.
2. Get a large mixing bowl: Toss in it the squash with 1 tsp of the spice mix.
3. Get a mixing bowl: Stir in it the flour with half of the remaining spice mix.
4. Get a mixing bowl: Stir in it the cornmeal with the remaining half of the spice mix.
5. Get a mixing bowl: Whisk in it the egg with milk.
6. Dust the squash slices with the flour mix then dip them in the milk mix followed by the cornmeal mix.
7. Place a large pan over medium heat. Heat in it 1 inch of oil. Cook in it the squash slices for 3 min until they become golden brown.
8. Serve your squash fries with your favorite sauce.
9. Enjoy.

JP's
COUSCOUS

🥣 Prep Time: 5 mins

🕐 Total Time: 10 mins

Servings per Recipe: 1

Calories	275.9
Fat	5.5g
Cholesterol	0.0mg
Sodium	379.1mg
Carbohydrates	45.0g
Protein	9.8g

Ingredients

1/3 C. couscous, uncooked
1/2 C. chicken broth
1 tsp olive oil

1/2 tsp Cajun seasoning
salt, to taste

Directions

1. Place a saucepan over medium heat. Stir in it the broth, olive oil, Cajun seasoning, and salt. Cook it until it starts boiling.
2. Turn off the heat and stir in the couscous. Put on the lid and let it sit for 6 min.
3. Serve your couscous warm.
4. Enjoy.

11-INGREDIENT
Jambalaya

Prep Time: 30 mins

Total Time: 1 hr 15 mins

Servings per Recipe: 4
Calories	439.1
Fat	17.1g
Cholesterol	32.3mg
Sodium	1526.0mg
Carbohydrates	55.3g
Protein	17.9g

Ingredients

rotisserie chicken, chopped
1/2 lb beef sausage, sliced
1 medium onion, of choice chopped
1 medium green bell pepper, chopped
1 tbsp minced garlic
2 cans Rotel Tomatoes
1 C. chicken broth
2 C. penne pasta, uncooked

1 tbsp Italian seasoning
1 tsp Cajun seasoning
2 stalks green onions, sliced

Directions

1. Place a large pot over medium heat. Cook in it the sausages for 8 min. Drain it and place it aside.
2. Stir the bell pepper with onion into the same pan and cook them for 5 min. Stir in the garlic and cook them for 2 min.
3. Add the chicken with cooked sausage to the pan with the remaining ingredients. Cook them until they start boiling.
4. Lower the heat and put on the lid. Cook the stew for 26 min. serve your stew warm.
5. Enjoy.

Louisianan
Trail Mix

Prep Time: 5 mins

Total Time: 20 mins

Servings per Recipe: 1	
Calories	734.4
Fat	32.5g
Cholesterol	0.0mg
Sodium	362.4mg
Carbohydrates	101.9g
Protein	17.8g

Ingredients

22 oz. boxes wheat squares
18.5 oz. boxes oat o's cereal
3.5 oz. packages pretzel sticks
1 box cheddar cheese crackers
1 C. roasted peanuts
1/2 C. canola oil

2 tbsp hot sauce
1/4 C. Cajun seasoning
1/4 C. garlic powder

Directions

1. Before you do anything, preheat the oven to 325 F.
2. Mix the wheat squares with cereal, pretzel sticks, cheese crackers and peanuts in a shallow baking pan.
3. Get a mixing bowl: Mix in it the oil with Cajun seasoning, garlic powder, and hot sauce. Add the mix to the cereal mix and toss them to coat.
4. Place the pan in the middle of the oven and let it cook for 16 min.
5. Allow your trail road mix to lose heat completely then serve it.
6. Enjoy.

BATON ROUGE
Bisque

Prep Time: 20 mins

Total Time: 50 mins

Servings per Recipe: 8	
Calories	431.7
Fat	31.5g
Cholesterol	145.7mg
Sodium	363.7mg
Carbohydrates	23.2g
Protein	16.7g

Ingredients

3 tbsp butter
3 tbsp all-purpose flour
1 tbsp vegetable oil
1 large onion, chopped
1 tbsp minced garlic
1 large celery, minced
Cajun seasoning
1 C. chicken broth
1 1/2 C. frozen corn kernels
1 bay leaf
2 C. milk

2 C. heavy cream
1 tsp liquid shrimp and crab boil seasoning
1 lb fresh lump crabmeat
1/4 C. chopped green onion
1/2 tsp Worcestershire sauce
salt and pepper
chopped green onion

Directions

1. Place a large heavy saucepan over medium heat.
2. Heat in it the butter. Add to it the flour and mix it well. Let it cook for 6 min while mixing it all the time. Turn off the heat.
3. Place a large pot over medium heat. Heat the oil in it. Sauté in it the onion, garlic, and celery for 2 min.
4. Stir in the Cajun seasoning with broth, corn, and bay leaf. Cook it until it starts simmering. Add the milk, cream, and liquid crab boil seasoning.
5. Bring the soup to a simmer then lower the heat and let it cook for 8 min. add the flour and butter mix gradually to the soup wile mixing all the time.
6. Let the soup cook for 10 min over low heat until it becomes thick. Add the crabmeat, green onions, and Worcestershire sauce.
7. Cook the soup for an extra 7 min. Adjust the seasoning of the chowder then serve it hot.
8. Enjoy.

Cajun
Aoli

🥣 Prep Time: 10 mins
🕐 Total Time: 10 mins

Servings per Recipe: 1
Calories   534.1
Fat   39.6g
Cholesterol   33.0mg
Sodium   931.3mg
Carbohydrates   38.9g
Protein   8.4g

Ingredients

1/2 C. mayonnaise
1/2 C. nonfat plain yogurt
1/2 tsp dried oregano
1/4 tsp garlic salt
1/4 tsp ground cumin

1/8 tsp cayenne pepper
1/8 tsp black pepper

Directions

1. Get a small mixing bowl: Whisk in it all the ingredients. Place the mayonnaise in the fridge until ready to serve.
2. Enjoy.

LOUISIANA X ARIZONA
Burgers

Prep Time: 10 mins
Total Time: 25 mins

Servings per Recipe: 4
Calories	263.3
Fat	8.8g
Cholesterol	66.0mg
Sodium	388.7mg
Carbohydrates	25.5g
Protein	20.2g

Ingredients

cooking spray
6 oz. ground turkey
6 oz. ground chicken
1 tbsp ketchup
1 tsp Worcestershire sauce
1/2 tsp Cajun seasoning
1/4 tsp hot sauce
1/2 red bell pepper, strips

4 slices onions, round slices
1 tbsp fat-free mayonnaise
1 tsp fat-free mayonnaise
2 tsp spicy brown mustard
4 small buns, slider style

Directions

1. Get a large mixing bowl: Mix in it the turkey, chicken, Ketchup, Worcestershire sauce, 1/2 tsp Cajun seasoning, and hot sauce, a pinch of salt and pepper.
2. Shape the mix into 4 burgers.
3. Place a large pan over medium heat. Heat a splash of oil in it. Cook in it the burgers for 5 min on each side with the lid on.
4. Get a small mixing bowl: Whisk in it the mayonnaise and mustard. Lay the mix over the bottom buns.
5. Place over them the burgers, onion slices, pepper strips and the top buns. Serve your burgers right away.
6. Enjoy.

Cajun Rice
Casserole

🥣 Prep Time: 10 mins

🕐 Total Time: 55 mins

Servings per Recipe: 10

Calories	374.1
Fat	9.0g
Cholesterol	62.6mg
Sodium	209.2mg
Carbohydrates	49.2g
Protein	24.3g

Ingredients

2 lbs ground turkey
1 large eggplant, peeled and chopped
1 onion, chopped
2 bell peppers, chopped
4 large garlic cloves, minced
1/2 C. green onion, chopped
2 C. chicken broth

1 tsp cayenne pepper, adjust to taste
1 tbsp season salt, to taste
3 C. brown rice, cooked

Directions

1. Place a large pan over medium heat. Cook in it the meat for 8 min. lower the heat.
2. Stir in the eggplant, onions, bell peppers, garlic and green onions. Put on the lid and let them cook for 16 min.
3. Stir in the broth with the cayenne pepper, a pinch of salt and pepper. Cook them until they start boiling.
4. Lower the heat and put on the lid. Cook the stew for 35 min. fold the cooked rice into the mix. Serve it warm.
5. Enjoy.

LOUISIANA
Corn Sauce

Prep Time: 5 mins
Total Time: 15 mins

Servings per Recipe: 4
Calories	56.9
Fat	5.8g
Cholesterol	15.2mg
Sodium	90.3mg
Carbohydrates	0.9g
Protein	0.4g

Ingredients
1/4 tsp chili powder
1/4 tsp black pepper
1/8 tsp garlic powder
1/8 tsp red pepper
2 tbsp butter

1 tsp cornstarch
1/4 C. chicken broth

Directions
1. Get a small mixing bowl: Whisk in it the broth with cornstarch until no lumps are found.
2. Place a heavy saucepan over medium heat. Stir in it the seasoning with butter and cook them for 60 sec.
3. Stir in the cornstarch mix and cook them until they start boiling. Cook the sauce over high heat until it becomes thick.
4. Turn off the heat and serve your sauce warm.
5. Enjoy.

Queen
Bean Soup

Prep Time: 10 mins
Total Time: 3 hr 40 mins

Servings per Recipe: 10
Calories	246.2
Fat	14.7g
Cholesterol	50.6mg
Sodium	49.6mg
Carbohydrates	9.6g
Protein	17.9g

Ingredients

1 (14 oz.) packages dry 18 bean soup mix
1/2 C. dried lentils
8 C. water
2 C. nonfat beef broth
1 lb stewing beef, cut into dices

3 tsp Cajun seasoning
salt

Directions

1. Place a large pot over high heat. Stir into it all the ingredients.
2. Put on the lid and let them cook for 3 h 30 min over low heat.
3. Adjust the seasoning of the soup then serve it hot.
4. Enjoy.

EMMA'S
Creole Frittata

Prep Time: 5 mins
Total Time: 15 mins

Servings per Recipe: 1
Calories	896.8
Fat	68.9g
Cholesterol	764.1mg
Sodium	2524.2mg
Carbohydrates	6.7g
Protein	59.8g

Ingredients

2 tsp butter
2 tsp peanut oil
3 eggs
1 tbsp water, lukewarm
creole seasoning, to taste
2 oz. turkey, chopped into small cubes
2 oz. smoked beef sausage, chopped into small cubes
2 tbsp onions, chopped

2 tbsp green bell peppers, chopped
1/4 tsp garlic, minced
2 oz. provolone cheese
fresh parsley, chopped
Louisiana hot sauce, to taste
1/2 C. creole tomato sauce

Directions

1. Place a large pan over medium heat. Cook in it the sausage, turkey, onions, and bell peppers. Cook them for 4 min.
2. Place a skillet over medium heat. Melt in it the butter with peanut oil.
3. Get a mixing bowl: Mix in it the water with eggs. Pour the mix in the heated pan and cook it for 1 to 2 min on each side.
4. Season omelet while it is in the pan with the creole seasoning then top it with the ham, sausage, onions, bell pepper, garlic and cheese.
5. Pull half of the omelet over the filling then cook it for an extra 2 min. Serve your omelet.
6. Enjoy.

Creole
Corn

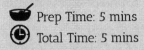 Prep Time: 5 mins

Total Time: 5 mins

Servings per Recipe: 10
Calories	182.8
Fat	9.4g
Cholesterol	20.3mg
Sodium	117.5mg
Carbohydrates	25.1g
Protein	4.1g

Ingredients

4 tbsp butter, cut into pieces
1 small garlic clove
1/8 tsp cayenne pepper
1/2 tsp paprika
1/8 tsp salt

1/2 tsp dried thyme
6 ears corn, freshly cooked

Directions

1. Get a blender: Place in it the butter with garlic, paprika, cayenne pepper, salt, and thyme. Blend them smooth.
2. Serve your sauce with cooked ears of corn.
3. Enjoy.

CREAMY CAJUN
Turkey Salad

Prep Time: 15 mins

Total Time: 30 mins

Servings per Recipe: 8

Calories	372.6
Fat	19.3g
Cholesterol	176.0mg
Sodium	381.1mg
Carbohydrates	38.9g
Protein	10.8g

Ingredients

1/2 lb rotini pasta
1 C. jennie-o cajun-style turkey, cooked and cut into bite size pieces
1 C. frozen peas
1 C. frozen corn
6 hard-boiled eggs, chopped
salt, to taste
fresh pepper, to taste
1/2 C. very finely chopped red onion

1 C. Miracle Whip
1/2 C. sour cream
1/2 C. whipping cream
2-3 tbsp honey mustard
2 tbsp sugar
2 tbsp apple cider vinegar

Directions

1. Prepare the pasta by following the instructions on the package.
2. Get a small mixing bowl: Whisk in it the miracle whip with cream, whipping cream, honey, sugar and vinegar to make the dressing.
3. Get a large mixing bowl: Toss in it the pasta with the dressing and the remaining ingredients.
4. Adjust the seasoning of the salad then serve it.
5. Enjoy.

Crunchy
Cajun Rolls

Prep Time: 10 mins
Total Time: 25 mins

Servings per Recipe: 8
Calories   363.1
Fat   7.6g
Cholesterol   62.4mg
Sodium   397.6mg
Carbohydrates   62.1g
Protein   12.6g

Ingredients

1/2 C. onion, chopped
1/4 C. green bell pepper, chopped
1/4 C. celery, chopped
1 tbsp garlic, minced
2 tbsp butter
3/4 C. mushroom, chopped
2 C. wild rice
2 C. water
1 tbsp Worcestershire sauce

2 tsp hot pepper sauce
1/2 tsp garlic powder
1/2 tsp cayenne pepper
1/2 tsp creole seasoning
16 oz. crescent rolls
1 egg, beaten
1/2 tsp garlic powder
1/8 tsp garlic salt

Directions

1. Before you do anything, preheat the oven to 375 F.
2. Place a large pan over medium heat. Melt the butter in it. Cook in it the onion, bell pepper, celery, garlic and mushrooms for 6 min.
3. Stir in the water with water, Worcestershire sauce, hot sauce, garlic powder, cayenne, and creole seasoning.
4. Cook them until they start boiling. Lower the heat and cook the mix for 12 min to make the filling. Place it aside to cool down completely.
5. Lay the crescent rolls on lined up baking sheet. Divide them into rectangular shapes.
6. Spoon some of the filling into the side of one rectangular. Fold the other half of dough over it and seal it.
7. Repeat the process with the remaining ingredients.
8. Get a small mixing bowl: Whisk in it the egg, garlic powder and garlic salt. Coat the rolls with the mix.
9. Place them in the oven and cook them for 14 min until they become golden brown.
10. Serve your crunchy rolls with your favorite dip.
11. Enjoy.

CAJUN CLAM
Chowder

Prep Time: 5 mins
Total Time: 15 mins

Servings per Recipe: 6
Calories	192.4
Fat	10.2g
Cholesterol	60.3mg
Sodium	523.1mg
Carbohydrates	6.1g
Protein	18.6g

Ingredients

1/4 C. vegetable oil
1/4 C. all-purpose flour
3-5 tsp Cajun seasoning
2 1/2 C. bottled clam juice
2 (14 1/2 oz.) cans diced tomatoes, in juice
1 (6 oz.) bags baby spinach leaves

2 tbsp chopped fresh thyme
1 garlic clove, pressed
1 lb lump crabmeat

Directions

1. Place a large pot over medium heat. Heat the oil in it. Add the flour and mix it well. Let it cook for 2 to 3 min until it becomes golden.
2. Mix in it the Cajun seasoning with a pinch of salt. Stir in the clam juice with tomato. Cook them for 4 min.
3. Stir in the spinach, thyme, and garlic. Let them cook for an extra 2 min.
4. Stir in the crabmeat and cook the stew for an extra 2 minutes. Serve your chowder hot.
5. Enjoy.

Hannah's
Macaroni Salad

🥣 Prep Time: 30 mins
🕐 Total Time: 40 mins

Servings per Recipe: 20
Calories	225.0
Fat	8.1g
Cholesterol	113.4mg
Sodium	684.1mg
Carbohydrates	20.5g
Protein	16.7g

Ingredients

1 (16 oz.) boxes cooked macaroni noodles
3 lbs medium unshelled shrimp
1 lb of real crabmeat
1/4 C. finely chopped red onion
1 C. mayonnaise
1 C. sour cream
1 tbsp spicy mustard
1/2 C. butter or 1/2 C. margarine
1 tbsp Cajun seasoning

1 tbsp Accent seasoning
1 tbsp Mrs. Dash seasoning mix
1 tsp onion powder
1/2 C. sweet relish
1/4 tsp cayenne pepper (optional)
1 tsp garlic powder

Directions

1. Cook the macaroni by following the directions on the package.
2. Place a large pan over medium heat. Heat in it the butter. Cook in it the garlic for 1 min.
3. Add the shrimp with Cajun seasoning then cook them for 4 min. Turn off the heat and stir in the crabmeat.
4. Get a large mixing bowl: Toss in it the macaroni with onion and mayo and sour cream.
5. Mix in the Onion powder, Garlic powder, Dash seasoning and Sweet Relish. Combine them well.
6. Stir the creamy shrimp mix into the salad. Place it in the fridge for at least 2 h then serve it.
7. Enjoy.

CAJUN
Crawfish Dip

Prep Time: 15 mins
Total Time: 40 mins

Servings per Recipe: 12
Calories	169.5
Fat	10.7g
Cholesterol	67.2mg
Sodium	925.2mg
Carbohydrates	4.9g
Protein	13.5g

Ingredients

2 garlic cloves, grated
1/2 C. scallion, thinly sliced, divided
1 tbsp butter
1 lb crawfish tail
1 lb processed cheese, block
20 oz. diced tomatoes with green chilies, drained

1/2 tsp kosher salt
1/4 tsp black pepper, freshly ground, to taste

Directions

1. Place a large pot over medium heat. Heat in it the butter. Cook in it the garlic with the white parts of scallions for 2 min.
2. Stir in the crawfish and let them cook for 6 min. Transfer the mix to a large mixing bowl.
3. Stir the tomato with cheese in the vacant pot. Cook them over medium heat for 2 to 3 min.
4. Add to them the crawfish mixture with a pinch of salt and pepper. Cook them for 3 to 4 min. Serve your dip warm.
5. Enjoy.

Cajun
Kale Lunch Box

Prep Time: 15 mins
Total Time: 35 mins

Servings per Recipe: 2	
Calories	749.3
Fat	55.5g
Cholesterol	0.0mg
Sodium	3683.5mg
Carbohydrates	46.9g
Protein	29.7g

Ingredients

2 bunches kale, teared
1 (14 oz.) packages extra firm tofu
2 tsps Cajun seasoning
1 C. carrot, matchsticks
2 eggs
4 C. water
1 tbsp vinegar, for poaching the egg
1/4 C. olive oil
1 tbsp sesame oil
3 tbsp tahini
2 tbsp cider vinegar

1 inch chunk gingerroot, finely chopped
1 tbsp homemade Cajun seasoning
1 tbsp sea salt
1 tbsp cayenne pepper
1 tbsp paprika
1 tbsp garlic powder
1 tbsp ground black pepper
2 tsps onion powder
2 tsps oregano
2 tsps thyme

Directions

1. Before you do anything, preheat the oven to 400 F.
2. Place the tofu on a kitchen towel and cover it with another one. Let it rest for 16 min.
3. Slice the tofu into long dices and toss them with 2 tsps of Cajun seasoning. Spread them on a lined up baking sheet.
4. Cook the tofu dices in the oven for 24 min. Place it aside to cool down.
5. Place a large saucepan of water over high heat. Heat it until it starts boiling. Blanch in it the kale for 3 min. Drain it and place it aside.
6. Place a saucepan over medium heat. Pour in it 4 C. of water with 1 tbsp of vinegar. Heat it until it starts simmering.
7. Crack each egg in a C. Use a wooden spoon to stir the water in around motion in one direction.
8. Add to it 1 egg at a time while stirring all the time. Turn the heat off and put on the lid. Let the eggs cook for 4 to 5 min.
9. Use a spoon to drain the poached eggs gently.
10. Get a mixing bowl: Whisk in it the dressing ingredients and place it aside.
11. Place the kale and carrot on 2 serving plates then top each one with tofu. Drizzle over them 1/4 C. of dressing and a poached egg.
12. Serve your breakfast plates right away. Enjoy.

CREOLE
Scrambled Eggs

Prep Time: 10 mins
Total Time: 30 mins

Servings per Recipe: 2
Calories	476.6
Fat	36.5g
Cholesterol	583.1mg
Sodium	755.4mg
Carbohydrates	9.9g
Protein	27.3g

Ingredients

1 packages turkey sausage, sliced
6 large eggs, beaten
1 tsp Cajun seasoning
2 tbsp olive oil
1 small red skin white potato, diced
1 small onion, chopped
1/2 medium green pepper, chopped

1/2 C. shredded Monterey jack pepper cheese
1/2 C. salsa

Directions

1. Get a large mixing bowl: Mix in it the eggs with Cajun spice.
2. Place a large pan over medium heat. Heat the olive oil in it. Cook in it the potato for 6 min.
3. Stir in the onion with pepper and cook them for another 6 min. Stir in the sliced sausage and cook them for 3 min.
4. Add the eggs mix and stir them well. Cook them for 3 to 4 minute while stirring it often.
5. Stir the cheese into the scramble until it melts. Serve it warm with salsa.
6. Enjoy.

Julia
Street Chowder

🥣 Prep Time: 10 mins
🕐 Total Time: 35 mins

Servings per Recipe: 1

Calories	524.5
Fat	19.4g
Cholesterol	286.4mg
Sodium	2620.9mg
Carbohydrates	42.0g
Protein	46.2g

Ingredients

1 tbsp olive oil
1/2 lb medium shrimp, peeled, de-veined
1/2 C. chopped onion
1/2 C. chopped green pepper
2 C. frozen Hash Browns, chopped slightly
1 cans chicken broth
2 tsps Cajun seasoning

2 tbsp all-purpose flour
2 tbsp water
1 cans diced tomatoes, undrained

Directions

1. Place a pot over medium heat. Heat the oil in it. Cook in it the shrimp, onion and green pepper for 4 min.
2. Stir in the Potatoes, broth and Cajun seasoning. Cook them until they start boiling. Lower the heat and let the soup cook for 24 min.
3. Get a small mixing bowl: Combine in it the water with flour. Stir them into the soup followed by the tomato.
4. Cook the soup for 6 min then serve it hot.
5. Enjoy.

ROYAL STREET
Meatball Stew

Prep Time: 45 mins
Total Time: 1 h 45 mins

Servings per Recipe: 6
Calories	765.9
Fat	55.7g
Cholesterol	167.7mg
Sodium	208.4mg
Carbohydrates	32.3g
Protein	33.3g

Ingredients

3/4 C. vegetable oil
1 C. all-purpose flour
3 C. onions, finely chopped
1 1/2 C. bell peppers, finely chopped
1 C. celery, finely chopped
water or beef broth
4 garlic cloves, minced
2 lbs ground chuck
2 large eggs
1/4 C. milk

1 tbsp Worcestershire sauce
1/2 C. fresh parsley, chopped
1/3 C. plain breadcrumbs
salt and cayenne pepper
1/4 C. green onion, chopped

Directions

1. Place a large pot over medium heat. Heat the oil in it. Mix the flour into it and cook it until it becomes golden brown.
2. Mix in it 2 C. of the chopped onion, 1 C. of the bell pepper and 1/2 C. of the celery. Cook them for 5 to 6 min.
3. Pour enough broth or water in the pot to fill 2/3 of it. Cook the soup until it starts boiling. Lower the heat and let it cook.
4. Get a large mixing bowl: Mix in it the ground chuck, remaining onions, bell pepper, and celery, 2 cloves of the minced garlic and eggs.
5. Add the milk with Worcestershire sauce, 1/4 C. of the parsley, bread crumbs, and salt and cayenne pepper then mix them well.
6. Shape the mix into bite size meatballs. Lower the meatballs into the pot and let them cook for 22 min without stirring them.
7. Add the cayenne pepper, rest of the garlic, parsley, green onion and a pinch of salt. Cook the stew for an extra 6 min.
8. Serve your stew hot with some rice. Enjoy.

Blackened
Potato Crusted Shrimp

Prep Time: 15 mins
Total Time: 25 mins

Servings per Recipe: 4
Calories	142.8
Fat	7.9g
Cholesterol	143.0mg
Sodium	642.5mg
Carbohydrates	1.7g
Protein	15.5g

Ingredients

1 lb jumbo shrimp, shelled and deveined
1 tsp blackening seasoning
2 C. frozen Hash Browns

2 tbsp vegetable oil
1 small lemon

Directions

1. Get a large mixing bowl: Toss in it the shrimp with Cajun blackening seasoning.
2. Place a large pan over medium heat. Heat the oil in it. Press the potato hash into the shrimp then cook them in the hot oil for 4 to 5 min on each side.
3. Squeeze over them some fresh lemon juice.
4. Enjoy.

CAJUN
Vanilla Pie

Prep Time: 25 mins
Total Time: 1 h 55 mins

Servings per Recipe: 8

Calories	420.9
Fat	14.7g
Cholesterol	89.5mg
Sodium	337.9mg
Carbohydrates	69.7g
Protein	4.6g

Ingredients

3 medium sweet potatoes, boiled and mashed
1/4 C. brown sugar
2 tbsp sugar
1 tbsp butter
1 tbsp pure vanilla extract
1 large egg
1 tbsp heavy cream
1/4 tsp ground cinnamon
1 pinch nutmeg
1 pinch ground allspice
1 9" unbaked pie shell

1/2 C. chopped pecans
3/4 C. granulated sugar
2 large eggs
3/4 C. dark corn syrup
1 tbsp butter, melted
1/2 tsp salt
ground cinnamon
2 tsps pure vanilla extract
whipped cream

Directions

1. Before you do anything, preheat the oven to 300 F.
2. Get a large mixing bowl: Beat in it the sweet potatoes, both sugars, butter, vanilla, egg, cinnamon, nutmeg, and allspice until they become smooth.
3. Spoon the mix into the pie crust. Garnish it with the pecans.
4. Get a mixing bowl: Mix in it the granulated sugar, eggs, corn syrup, melted butter, salt, cinnamon and vanilla.
5. Sprinkle the mix over the pecan layer. Place the pie in the oven and let it cook for 1 h 32 min.
6. Allow the pie to cool down completely then serve it with your favorite toppings.
7. Enjoy.

French Quarter
Green Beans

🥄 Prep Time: 30 mins
🕐 Total Time: 1 h 30 mins

Servings per Recipe: 6
Calories	438.8
Fat	29.9g
Cholesterol	85.7mg
Sodium	837.1mg
Carbohydrates	27.9g
Protein	18.1g

Ingredients

4 slices thick-sliced turkey bacon, cut into pieces
2 small onions, chopped
2 garlic cloves
3 lbs green beans
1/4 C. butter
1 pinch of grated nutmeg
1/2 C. all-purpose flour
1/2 C. heavy cream
1 1/2 C. grated white cheddar cheese
4 C. chicken broth
salt and pepper
2 (6 oz.) cans fried onions

Directions

1. Before you do anything, preheat the oven to 350 F.
2. Place a Dutch oven over medium heat. Cook in it the bacon for 5 min. Stir into it the onion and cook them for 7 min.
3. Stir in the garlic and cook them for 2 min. Place it aside.
4. Stir in the green beans with enough broth or water to cover it in a large saucepan.
5. Lower the heat put on the lid. Let the mix cook for 30 min. drain the beans and reserve the cooking liquid.
6. Place a large pan over medium heat. Heat in it the butter until it melts. Sauté in it the rest of the onion with salt and nutmeg. Place it aside.
7. Cook them for 7 min. Mix in the flour followed by the cream and the reserved bean cooking liquid. Cook it for 6 min until it mixture becomes thick.
8. Add the cheese and green beans and cook them for few minutes until the cheese melts.
9. Pour the mix into a glass casserole dish. Place it in the oven and let it cook for 26 min. spread the onion and bacon mix on top.
10. Bake it for an extra 14 min. Serve it hot.
11. Enjoy.

HOUMA
Potato Pots

Prep Time: 20 mins
Total Time: 1 h 50 mins

Servings per Recipe: 2
Calories	642.4
Fat	32.5g
Cholesterol	375.2mg
Sodium	1689.0mg
Carbohydrates	37.3g
Protein	49.4g

Ingredients
1 lb jumbo shrimp, deveined
2 large baking potatoes
1 C. guacamole
3 tbsp Cajun seasoning
2 tbsp minced garlic

1/2 C. sour cream
1 C. shredded cheddar cheese

Directions
1. Before you do anything, preheat the grill.
2. Place each potato in the middle of piece of foil and wrap it around it. Place it on the grill and let them cook until they become slightly soft.
3. Toss the shrimp with Cajun seasoning and garlic in a shallow roasting pan. Place the pan over the grill on the indirect side of it.
4. Let the shrimp cook for 12 min. Flip it and let cook for another 12 min.
5. Once the shrimp and potato are done place them aside to lose heat for a while.
6. Discard the foil sheets and slice them in half. Spoon some of the potato flesh to leave 1/4 of it only.
7. Place 4 shrimp aside. Chop the remaining shrimp and place it in the potato shells followed by the cheese.
8. Place each one of them in a foil packet. Place them over the grill and let them cook for an extra 12 min.
9. Place the 4 shrimps in a small foil packet and grill them for 6 min.
10. Once the time is up, top the shrimp layer with guacamole and sour cream. Garnish them with the whole remaining 4 shrimps. Serve them right away.
11. Enjoy.

Baked Sole
with Cauliflower Salad

🥣 Prep Time: 10 mins
🕐 Total Time: 40 mins

Servings per Recipe: 2
Calories	744.6
Fat	14.0g
Cholesterol	328.2mg
Sodium	1111.4mg
Carbohydrates	22.8g
Protein	129.0g

Ingredients

8 sole fillets
3 C. French style green beans
3 C. cauliflower, florets
1 tbsp butter
1/8 C. lemon juice

1 green onion
salt
pepper
Cajun seasoning

Directions

1. Before you do anything, preheat the oven to 350 F.
2. Place the sole fillets on a greased baking pan. Drizzle over them the fresh lemon juice followed by the Cajun seasoning.
3. Place the sole sheet in the oven and let it cool for 32 min.
4. Place the cauliflower in a heatproof bowl. Cook it in the microwave for 9 min.
5. Get a heatproof bowl: Stir in it the green beans with green onion. Cook them in the microwave for 9 min.
6. Drain the coked veggies. Add to them the butter with a pinch of salt and pepper. Toss them to coat.
7. Serve your baked sole with the veggies salad.
8. Enjoy.

CREOLE
Country Hens

Prep Time: 10 mins
Total Time: 24 h 10 mins

Servings per Recipe: 4

Calories	1602.6
Fat	107.1g
Cholesterol	756.2mg
Sodium	389.7mg
Carbohydrates	20.1g
Protein	129.3g

Ingredients

4 oz. hot smoked beef sausage, chopped
1/2 C. long grain white rice
1 cans diced tomatoes
1/2 C. sliced green onion
1/4 C. chopped green bell pepper
1 garlic clove, minced
1/4 tsp dried thyme leaves

4 Cornish hens
1 tbsp butter, melted

Directions

1. Place a pot over medium heat. Cook in it the sausages for 8 min. add the rice and let them cook for 3 min.

2. Stir in the tomatoes, onions, pepper, garlic and thyme. Cook them until they start boiling. Put on the lid and let them cook for 22 min.

3. Spoon the mix into the cavity of the hens. Place them in a greased roasting pan and coat them with butter, a pinch of salt and pepper.

4. Place them in the oven and let them cook for 60 min. allow them to rest for 5 min then serve them warm.

5. Enjoy.

Lake Charles
Avocado Glazed Kabobs

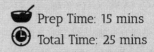 Prep Time: 15 mins

Total Time: 25 mins

Servings per Recipe: 2
Calories	525.3
Fat	47.7g
Cholesterol	85.6mg
Sodium	482.4mg
Carbohydrates	18.0g
Protein	11.7g

Ingredients

20 large uncooked prawns, peeled and deveined
2 tbsp Cajun seasoning
2 tsps ground cumin
1 tsp dried oregano
2 garlic cloves, crushed
50 ml olive oil
1 large avocado

2 tbsp sour cream
2 tbsp mayonnaise
1 tsp Tabasco sauce
1/2 tsp garlic powder
1 tbsp fresh coriander, chopped
1 tbsp lemon juice

Directions

1. Get a large mixing bowl: Stir in it the prawns with Cajun seasoning, oregano, cumin, garlic, olive oil, a pinch of salt and pepper.
2. Place the mix in the fridge to sit for at least 30 min.
3. Before you do anything, preheat the grill and grease it.
4. Drain the prawns and thread them into skewers. Place them on the grill and cook them for 4 to 5 min on each side.
5. Get a blender: Place in it all the avocado sauce ingredients. Blend them smooth.
6. Serve your skewers warm with the avocado sauce.
7. Enjoy.

CAJUN
Pilaf

Prep Time: 10 mins

Total Time: 30 mins

Servings per Recipe: 2

Calories	530.8
Fat	5.9g
Cholesterol	127.8mg
Sodium	514.2mg
Carbohydrates	70.5g
Protein	45.0g

Ingredients

cooking spray
1 small brown onion, chopped
2 celery ribs, chopped
2 garlic cloves, crushed
1/4 tsp ground cinnamon
2 cloves
1/4 tsp ground turmeric

3/4 C. long-grain white rice
2 C. chicken stock
1/4 C. flat leaf parsley, chopped
360 g white fish fillets
2 tsps Cajun seasoning

Directions

1. Place a pot over medium heat. Heat the oil in it. Add the onion, celery and garlic. Let them cook for 6 min.
2. Stir in the seasonings and cook them for 1 min. Stir in the rice and cook them for an extra 2 min.
3. Pour in the broth and cook them until they start boiling. Lower the heat and put on the lid. Cook the pilaf for 22 min.
4. Fold the parsley into the pilaf.
5. Place a large pan over medium heat. Heat a splash of oil in it.
6. Season the fish fillets with Cajun spice, a pinch of salt and pepper. Cook them in the hot oil for 4 to 6 min on each side.
7. Serve your fish fillets warm with the pilaf.
8. Enjoy.

Cajun
Tortillas Pan

Prep Time: 20 mins
Total Time: 50 mins

Servings per Recipe: 4
Calories   407.5
Fat   18.1g
Cholesterol   73.4mg
Sodium   1131.2mg
Carbohydrates   36.7g
Protein   24.4g

Ingredients

2 tbsp butter
1/2 C. green bell pepper, chopped
1/2 C. onion, chopped
2 jalapeno peppers, chopped
4 oz. green chilies, chopped
10 oz. condensed cream of chicken soup
10 oz. Rotel tomatoes & chilies

2 C. cooked chicken, cubes
6 flour tortillas, chopped
1 1/2 C. shredded cheddar cheese
sour cream
green onion
sliced avocado

Directions

1. Before you do anything, preheat the oven to 325 F.
2. Place a pot over medium heat. Heat in it the butter. Sauté in it the onion with pepper and jalapenos for 6 min.
3. Stir in the green chiles, soup, Rotel tomatoes, and chicken.
4. Lay 1/3 of the tortillas in a greased baking dish. Spread over it 1/3 of the chicken mix followed by 1/3 of the cheese.
5. Repeat the process to make an extra 2 layers. Place the pan in the oven and let it cook for 35 min. serve it hot.
6. Enjoy.

CREOLE SUMMER
Watermelon Relish

Prep Time: 30 mins

Total Time: 55 mins

Servings per Recipe: 40
Calories	25.0
Fat	0.0g
Cholesterol	0.0mg
Sodium	175.8mg
Carbohydrates	5.7g
Protein	0.1g

Ingredients

5 C. watermelon rind, diced
1 large onion, diced
1 red bell pepper, diced
1 green bell pepper, diced
1-2 fresh jalapeno pepper, sliced
1 C. sugar
2 C. vinegar
1 tbsp pickling salt

1/2 tsp mustard, seed
1 bay leaf
1 tsp celery seed
1 tsp peppercorns
1 tsp pepper, flakes

Directions

1. Get a large mixing bowl: Stir in it the onion with rind, peppers, and salt. Pour over them enough cold water to cover them.
2. Place the bowl in the fridge and let it sit for an overnight.
3. Get a large pot. Stir in it the sugar with vinegar, mustard, bay leaf, celery seed, peppercorns, and pepper flakes.
4. Cook them over medium heat until they start boiling. Drain the rind and onion mix then stir it into the pot.
5. Cook them until they start boiling again. Lower the heat and bring to a simmer.
6. Spoon the mix into sterilized jars leaving 1/2 of space empty in each jar. Seal the jars and place them in some hot water for 12 min.
7. Let them sit for at least 1 week before serving it.
8. Enjoy.

Creole
Stuffed Peppers

🥄 Prep Time: 45 mins
🕐 Total Time: 1 h 45 mins

Servings per Recipe: 6

Calories	636.9
Fat	32.2g
Cholesterol	105.8mg
Sodium	1325.7mg
Carbohydrates	54.6g
Protein	32.1g

Ingredients

6 - 10 large bell peppers, tops and insides removed
4 C. cooked rice
24 - 32 oz. tomato sauce
1 cans diced tomatoes & chilies
1 large onion, chopped
1 medium bell pepper, chopped

1 - 2 tbsp minced garlic
Cajun seasoning
1 lb ground beef
1 lb ground turkey sausage

Directions

1. Before you do anything, preheat the oven to 350 F.
2. Place a large pan over medium heat. Cook in it the ground beef and ground sausage for 10 min. discard the excess grease.
3. Stir in the seasonings, veggies, diced tomatoes, and tomato sauce. Cook them until the veggies are soft. Drain 2 C. of sauce from the mix and place it aside.
4. Stir in the rice into the pan and turn off the heat to make the filling. Spoon the mix into the bell peppers.
5. Place them in a greased casserole dish. Pour the reserve sauce all over it. Cook it in the oven for 60 min.
6. Serve your stuffed peppers warm.
7. Enjoy.

...N Gumbo

Prep Time: 40 mins
Total Time: 1 h 25 mins

Servings per Recipe: 6

Calories	1201.9
Fat	76.6g
Cholesterol	167.2mg
Sodium	1645.3mg
Carbohydrates	69.0g
Protein	55.2g

Ingredients

1/4 C. all-purpose flour
1 tsp salt
1/2 tsp black pepper
1/4 tsp cayenne
1 tsp paprika
1/2 tsp onion powder
1/2 tsp garlic powder
6 chicken breasts, cubed
1/4 C. vegetable oil
1 C. all-purpose flour

1 C. lard
2 C. chopped onions
1 1/2 C. chopped green bell peppers
1 1/2 C. chopped celery
2 quarts chicken stock
3/4 lb beef sausage, cubed
2 garlic cloves, minced
3 C. cooked rice

Directions

1. Get a large mixing bowl: Toss in it the spices with chicken and 1/4 C. of flour.
2. Place a large pan over medium heat. Heat the oil in it. Add the chicken in batches and coo them for 5 min per batch.
3. Place a pot over medium heat. Melt the lard in it. Add the flour and mix it well then cook it until it becomes golden brown.
4. Add the veggies and mix them well. Add to it the stock gradually while mixing them all the time.
5. Cook them until they start boiling. Stir in the chicken, sausage, and garlic. Lower the heat and let the stew cook for 60 min.
6. Adjust the seasoning of your gumbo then serve it warm.
7. Enjoy.

Quick
Cajun Gumbo

Prep Time:
Total Time:

Servings per Recipe: 8
Calories	475.9
Fat	24.9g
Cholesterol	77.2mg
Sodium	963.7mg
Carbohydrates	39.4g
Protein	21.2g

Ingredients
1 box Zatarians gumbo base mix
1 lb chicken
1 lb smoked sausage
1 boxes sliced frozen okra, defrosted

2 C. long grain white rice
1/2 tbsp salt

Directions
1. Cook the rice by following the instructions on the package.
2. Prepare the gumbo mix by following the instructions on the package.
3. Pour the mix into a large pot over high heat. Cook it until it starts boiling while stirring it all the time.
4. Stir in the meat and cook them until they start boiling again. Lower the heat and let the stew coo for 30 min while stirring it from time to time.
5. Add the okra and cook them until they start boiling again. Serve your gumbo with white rice.
6. Enjoy.

CREOLE
Crab Cakes

Prep Time: 30 mins

Total Time: 40 mins

Servings per Recipe: 8

Calories	173.2
Fat	6.1g
Cholesterol	115.6mg
Sodium	378.7mg
Carbohydrates	17.3g
Protein	13.2g

Ingredients

2 roasted red peppers
1/2 C. fat-free mayonnaise
1/4-1/2 tsp cayenne pepper
1/2 tsp seasoning salt
3 tsps olive oil, divided
1/2 onion, chopped
1 stalk celery, chopped
2 eggs, beaten
2 tbsp ground walnuts
2 tbsp chopped fresh parsley
2 tbsp fat-free mayonnaise
1 tbsp lemon juice

1 tsp Cajun seasoning
1/2 tsp crab boil seasoning
2 tsps Worcestershire sauce
1/2 tsp mustard powder
1/4 tsp crushed celery seed
1/2 tsp ground paprika
1 lb crawfish meat or 1 lb crabmeat
1/2-1 tsp hot pepper sauce
1 C. whole wheat breadcrumbs

Directions

1. Get a food processor: Place in it the roasted peppers then process them until they become smooth.
2. Pour in the mayonnaise and spices then blend them smooth to make the sauce. Place it in the fridge.
3. Get a large mixing bowl: Combine in it all the ingredients except for the bread crumbs. Shape the mix into 8 cakes then roll them in the breadcrumbs.
4. Place a large pan over medium heat. Heat 2 tsps of olive oil. Cook in it the fish cakes for 3 to 4 min on each side.
5. Serve your fish cakes warm with the pepper sauce.
6. Enjoy.

Baton Rouge
Cabbage Stew

🥣 Prep Time: 20 mins
🕐 Total Time: 35 mins

Servings per Recipe: 12
Calories   111.9
Fat   1.8g
Cholesterol   0.0mg
Sodium   701.8mg
Carbohydrates   22.3g
Protein   5.1g

Ingredients

26 oz. pasta sauce
26 oz. extra mild salsa
1 lb ground meat
2 large heads of cabbage
salt and pepper

8 oz. water or 8 oz. chicken stock

Directions

1. Bring a large salted pot of water to a boil. Core the cabbage and slice it into 1/2 inch thick slices.
2. Cook them in the hot water for 3 to 4 min until they wilt.
3. Place a pot over medium heat. Cook in it the meat for 8 min. Discard the excess grease. Rinse the cooked meat and drain it.
4. Stir the cooked meat back in the pot with sauce, and salsa to wilted cabbage. Let it cook for 8 min.
5. Serve your un-rolled cabbage stew warm.
6. Enjoy.

SPICY
Mayo Salad

 Prep Time: 10 mins

Total Time: 10 mins

Servings per Recipe: 8
Calories	404.0
Fat	22.3g
Cholesterol	7.6mg
Sodium	746.6mg
Carbohydrates	50.7g
Protein	5.2g

Ingredients
3 cans corn, drained
2 C. shredded cheddar cheese
1 small purple onion, diced
1 medium bell pepper, sliced
1 C. Hellmann's mayonnaise

1 (11 1/2 oz.) bag Fritos corn chips
lots cracked black pepper

Directions
1. Get a large mixing bowl: Stir in it the corn with cheese, onion, pepper, and mayonnaise.
2. Place the salad in the fridge for few hours.
3. Top the salad with the Fritos chips.
4. Enjoy.

Creole
Spring Rolls

Prep Time: 30 mins
Total Time: 40 mins

Servings per Recipe: 10
Calories	361.5
Fat	14.1g
Cholesterol	29.1mg
Sodium	630.0mg
Carbohydrates	43.6g
Protein	15.8g

Ingredients

1/2 lb beef sausage, diced
6 cloves garlic, minced
1 medium onion, minced
1 cans black beans
1 avocado, diced
1/4 lb cheddar cheese, grated
2 tbsp fresh cilantro, chopped
1 ear corn, roasted

1 roasted red bell pepper
1 pinch cumin
1 pinch chili powder
salt and pepper
15-20 eggroll wraps
oil

Directions

1. Place a large pan over medium heat. Cook in it the sausage for 5 min. add the onion with garlic and cook them for 10 min to make the filling.
2. Turn off the heat and spoon the mix into a mixing bowl to cool down.
3. Lay a wrapper on a working surface with the pointed corner facing towards you. Brush its edges with some water.
4. Place 3 tbsp of the filling in the middle of the wrapper then pull the pointed corner on top of it and press it to seal it.
5. Brush the right and left corner over the filling and press them to seal them.
6. Repeat the process with the remaining ingredients.
7. Place a large pan over medium heat. Heat in it 1 inch of oil. Cook in it the rolls in the batches until they become golden brown.
8. Serve your crunchy rolls with your favorite sauce.
9. Enjoy.

SHREVEPORT
Stew

Prep Time: 20 mins

Total Time: 1 h 20 mins

Servings per Recipe: 8

Calories	431.4
Fat	18.3g
Cholesterol	199.6mg
Sodium	1415.0mg
Carbohydrates	21.5g
Protein	44.9g

Ingredients

1 tsp olive oil
1 lb Italian turkey sausage
1 lb white fish fillet, chunks
1 lb sea scallops
1 lb shrimp
2 red bell peppers, chopped
2 stalks celery, chopped
1 large onion, chopped

1 tbsp basil leaves, crushed
1 tbsp oregano leaves, crushed
2-3 cloves garlic, crushed
4 cans diced tomatoes

Directions

1. Place a Dutch oven over medium heat. Cook in it the sausage for 8 min.
2. Stir in the Basil, oregano and Garlic, onion, celery& pepper. Cook them for 22 min.
3. Stir in the tomato and let them cook for an extra 22 min. Fold the seafood into the mix and let them cook for 6 to 8 min until they are done.
4. Serve your stew hot with some pasta.
5. Enjoy.

Southern
Lunch Box
(Spicy Corn Salad)

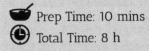 Prep Time: 10 mins

Total Time: 8 h

Servings per Recipe: 6

Calories	269.9
Fat	20.7g
Cholesterol	1.2mg
Sodium	331.2mg
Carbohydrates	21.8g
Protein	3.2g

Ingredients

17 1/2 oz. cook frozen kernel corn
1 green bell pepper, diced
1 red bell pepper, diced
1 C. hot pickled okra or 6 green onions
1/2 C. parsley, minced
1 C. cherry tomatoes, halved
Tabasco:
1 tsp sugar
1/4 C. wine vinegar
1 tsp creole mustard

1 tbsp dried basil leaves
2 tbsp mayonnaise
1/2 tsp black pepper
1/2 tsp Tabasco sauce
salt
1/2 C. olive oil

Directions

1. Get a large mixing bowl: Stir in it all the salad ingredients.
2. Get a small mixing bowl: Whisk in it the sauce ingredients except of the oil.
3. Add to it the olive oil in a steady stream while whisking it all the time. Drizzle the sauce over the salad.
4. Place it in the fridge for an overnight then serve it.
5. Enjoy.

CREOLE
Seafood Fillets

Prep Time: 5 mins
Total Time: 15 mins

Servings per Recipe: 2
Calories	435.4
Fat	3.9g
Cholesterol	198.1mg
Sodium	544.6mg
Carbohydrates	10.2g
Protein	84.3g

Ingredients
4 fish fillets
butter-flavored cooking spray
2 tsps Cajun seasoning
1/4 C. seasoned breadcrumbs

salt and pepper

Directions
1. Before you do anything, preheat the oven to 400 F.
2. Place the fish fillets on a lined up baking sheet. Grease them with a cooking spray.
3. Season them with the Cajun spice then top them with the bread crumbs.
4. Place the fish pan in the oven. Cook it in the oven for 4 to 6 min. Serve it warm.
5. Enjoy.

Creole
Alfredo

Prep Time: 5 mins

Total Time: 4 h 5 mins

Servings per Recipe: 4
Calories	763.0
Fat	48.6g
Cholesterol	227.6mg
Sodium	2723.5mg
Carbohydrates	14.8g
Protein	64.6g

Ingredients

1 1/2-2 lbs boneless skinless chicken
garlic soup mix
8 oz. cream cheese
1 cans cream of chicken soup
1 cans cream of mushroom soup
1 cans water
2 chicken bouillon cubes

1-2 tbsp Cajun seasoning
1/4 tsp lemon pepper
canned mushroom
8 oz. parmesan cheese
linguine

Directions

1. Stir the chicken with soup mix, cream cheese, mushroom soup, water, bouillon cubes, Cajun seasoning, lemon pepper, some canned mushroom, a pinch of salt and pepper.
2. In a greased slow cooker. Put on the lid and let them cook for 4 h on low.
3. Stir in the cheese until it melts. Serve your Alfredo sauce with some pasta.
4. Enjoy.

Rolls

Servings per Recipe: 4

Calories	566.6
Fat	15.4g
Cholesterol	76.2mg
Sodium	759.1mg
Carbohydrates	67.0g
Protein	38.1g

Ingredients

500 g beef rump, sliced
1 yellow onion, sliced
1 red capsicum, sliced
2 tbsp Cajun seasoning

3 medium tomatoes, wedges
1 French baguette
lettuce leaf

Directions

1. Place a large pan over medium heat. Heat the oil in it. Cook in it the beef for 8 min. Drain it and place it aside.
2. Sauté in it the onion with capsicum and seasoning for 5 min in the same pan.
3. Stir in the tomato wedges and cook them for 16 min over low heat. Add the browned beef to the pan.
4. Slice the baguette open and lay in it the lettuce leaves. Spoon over it the beef mix. Serve it with your favorite toppings.
5. Enjoy.

Lemon
Creole Chicken

🥄 Prep Time: 10 mins
🕐 Total Time: 50 mins

Servings per Recipe: 6
Calories	203.9
Fat	13.8g
Cholesterol	69.0mg
Sodium	313.0mg
Carbohydrates	1.9g
Protein	17.2g

Ingredients
1/2 C. lemon juice
1/4 C. hot pepper sauce
3 tbsp Cajun seasoning

2 lbs chicken

Directions
1. Before you do anything, preheat the oven to 350 F.
2. Stir all the ingredients in a greased baking dish.
3. Place it in the oven and let it cook for 48 min. serve your chicken casserole warm.
4. Enjoy.

HOMEMADE
Spicy Mustard

Prep Time: 15 mins

Total Time: 15 mins

Servings per Recipe: 1

Calories	851.0
Fat	43.4g
Cholesterol	0.0mg
Sodium	38.9mg
Carbohydrates	93.4g
Protein	34.3g

Ingredients

2 oz. dry mustard
1 tbsp flour
3 tbsp malt vinegar
1 tbsp honey
1 clove garlic, chopped
1 tbsp hot pepper flakes
1 tsp cumin

1 tsp thyme
1 tsp black pepper
1 tsp paprika

Directions

1. Get a mixing bowl: Stir in it the flour with mustard. Add to it 1/4 C. of cold water while mixing them all the time.

2. Let the mustard sauce sit for 16 min. add the rest of the ingredients and mix them well. Serve your sauce whenever you desire.

3. Enjoy.

Creole
Pizza

🍲 Prep Time: 30 mins
🕐 Total Time: 1 h

Servings per Recipe: 4
Calories   611.9
Fat   37.6g
Cholesterol   115.5mg
Sodium   1530.6mg
Carbohydrates   33.1g
Protein   37.2g

Ingredients

1 large pizza crusts
1/2 lb beef sausage, cooked, crumbled
2 chicken breasts, cooked, strips
1 small zucchini, sliced
1 red bell pepper, diced
1/2 C. chopped onion
2 cloves chopped garlic
1 cans tomato sauce
1 cans diced tomatoes
1 tbsp brown mustard

1 tbsp chopped fresh ginger
2 tsps brown sugar
2 tsps Worcestershire sauce
2 tsps cumin
2 tsps other Cajun seasoning
1/2 tsp oregano
1 dash hot sauce, to taste
8 oz. grated cheese

Directions

1. Before you do anything, preheat the oven to 350 F.
2. Get a food processor: Combine in it the onions, tomato sauce, tomatoes, brown sugar, garlic, ginger, and all the seasonings.
3. Pulse them several times until they become puréed to make the sauce.
4. Transfer the sauce to a heavy saucepan. Let it cook for 35 min.
5. Place the pizza crust on a lined up baking sheet. Top it wit half of the sauce followed by the zucchini slices and chicken.
6. Top them with the sausage and bell peppers. Drizzle the remaining sauce on top with cheese.
7. Place the pizza in the oven and let it cook for 16 min. serve it hot.
8. Enjoy.

CREOLE
Shrimp Tortillas

Prep Time: 30 mins

Total Time: 40 mins

Servings per Recipe: 8
Calories	306.6
Fat	6.9g
Cholesterol	86.4mg
Sodium	469.2mg
Carbohydrates	42.1g
Protein	17.3g

Ingredients

1/2 C. uncooked rice
1 tbsp olive oil
1 lb uncooked medium shrimp, peeled
and deveined
1 small red onion, chopped
1 tbsp minced garlic
2 tsps Cajun seasoning

1 C. tomato sauce
8 8-inch flour tortillas, warmed

Directions

1. Cook the rice by following the instructions on the package.
2. Place a large pan over medium heat. Heat the oil in it. Cook in it the shrimp, onion, garlic, and Cajun seasoning for 4 min.
3. Mix in it the pasta sauce with cooked rice. Divide the mix between the tortillas and wrap them. Serve them right away.
4. Enjoy.

Creole
Ice Cream

Prep Time: 3 hr
Total Time: 6 hr

Servings per Recipe: 1 carton
Calories	3547.7
Fat	269.6g
Cholesterol	1669.5mg
Sodium	608.2mg
Carbohydrates	261.3g
Protein	40.2g

Ingredients

2 1/2 C. heavy cream
1 C. whole milk
3/4 C. dark brown sugar
5 egg yolks
1 C. sweet potato puree, canned
1/4 tsp ground nutmeg
3/4 tsp ground cinnamon

1/2 tsp cayenne pepper
1 1/2 tbsp dried rosemary
1/4 C. pecans, lightly chopped

Directions

1. Place a heavy saucepan over medium heat. Stir in it the cream, milk, and brown sugar until they become hot.
2. Get a mixing bowl: Beat in it the eggs while adding 1 C. hot cream mix gradually. Stir the mix into the saucepan gradually while mixing all the time.
3. Let it cook over medium heat while stirring all the time until it becomes slightly thick for 7 min.
4. Once the again, pour the mix into a large mixing bowl. Add to it the sweet potato puree, nutmeg, cinnamon, cayenne pepper and rosemary. Mix them well.
5. Cover the bowl with a plastic wrap and place it in the fridge for 2 h 30 min.
6. Once the time is up, prepare the ice cream by following the manufacturer's instructions. Serve it with your favorite toppings.
7. Enjoy.

CAJUN
Sausage Kabobs

Prep Time: 10 mins
Total Time: 25 mins

Servings per Recipe: 4
Calories	333.5
Fat	23.6g
Cholesterol	48.8mg
Sodium	1038.6mg
Carbohydrates	12.3g
Protein	17.7g

Ingredients
1 beef sausages, sliced
1 green bell pepper, chopped
1 red bell pepper, chopped
1 yellow bell pepper, chopped
1 onion, diced

1 tbsp Cajun seasoning
skewer

Directions
1. Before you do anything, preheat the grill and grease it.
2. Thread the sausage slices with bell peppers and onion into the skewers while alternating between them.
3. Season them with the Cajun seasoning, a pinch of salt and pepper. Cook the kabobs on the grill for 16 min or until they are done.
4. Serve your kabobs with your favorite sauce.
5. Enjoy.

Creole
Shrimp Bites

Prep Time: 45 mins
Total Time: 1 hr 4 mins

Servings per Recipe: 1
Calories   62.6
Fat   2.1g
Cholesterol   30.6mg
Sodium   186.2mg
Carbohydrates   7.3g
Protein   3.2g

Ingredients

2 tbsp parsley, minced
2 tbsp green onions, minced
2 tbsp butter
2 tbsp flour
1/2 C. milk
1/2 tsp salt

1/4 tsp hot pepper sauce
1/2 lb shrimp, cooked
2 eggs
2 C. breadcrumbs
oil, for frying

Directions

1. Place a saucepan over medium heat. Heat in it the butter. Add the green onions with parsley and cook them for 1 min.
2. Add the flour and mix them well. Pour in the milk with hot sauce and a pinch of salt. Whisk them until they become smooth.
3. Let them cook until they become thick. Turn off the heat and fold the shrimp into the mix.
4. Allow the mix to cool down for a while then shape it into bite size balls.
5. Whisk the eggs in a shallow bowl. Lower in it the shrimp balls then coat them with the bread crumbs, dip them again in the eggs and roll them in the breadcrumbs.
6. Place them on a lined up baking sheet. Place the shrimp balls in the fridge and let them sit for 32 min.
7. Place a large skillet over medium heat. Heat 1/4 to 1/2 inch of oil in it. Add the shrimp balls and cook them for 4 min until they become golden brown.
8. Drain the shrimp balls then serve them with your favorite dip.
9. Enjoy.

CREOLE
Fried Crabs

Prep Time: 15 mins

Total Time: 45 mins

Servings per Recipe: 4
Calories	360.5
Fat	16.2g
Cholesterol	61.0mg
Sodium	1469.2mg
Carbohydrates	27.0g
Protein	26.0g

Ingredients

3 tsps canola oil, divided
1 small onion, finely diced
1/2 C. finely diced green bell pepper
1/2 C. frozen corn kernels, thawed
1 1/2 tsps Cajun seasoning, divided
1 lb pasteurized crabmeat
1 large egg white
3/4 C. plain breadcrumbs
1/4 C. mayonnaise
1/2 tsp grated lemon zest

1/4 C. mayonnaise
2 tbsp sour cream
2 scallions, chopped
2 tsps capers
1 tbsp Dijon mustard
1 tbsp sweet relish
1/4 tsp ground pepper

Directions

1. Before you do anything, preheat the oven to 425 F.
2. Place a large pan over medium heat. Heat in it 1 tsp of oil. Sauté in it the onion, bell pepper, corn and 1 tsp Cajun seasoning for 5 mins.
3. Drain them and transfer them to a mixing bowl. Let it sit for 6 min. Mix in the crab, egg white, 1/2 C. breadcrumbs, mayonnaise and lemon zest.
4. Shape the mix into 8 cakes and place them on a lined up baking pan.
5. Get a small mixing bowl: Stir in it 1/4 C. breadcrumbs, 1/2 tsp Cajun seasoning and 2 tsps oil. Press the mix into the crab cakes.
6. Cook them in the oven for 22 min.
7. To make the sauce: mayonnaise, sour cream, scallions, capers, mustard, relish and pepper. Serve it with the crab cakes.
8. Get a mixing bowl: Whisk in it the
9. Enjoy.

Spicy
Ginger Cake

🥄 Prep Time: 10 mins
🕐 Total Time: 45 mins

Servings per Recipe: 12
Calories	387.0
Fat	19.2g
Cholesterol	65.7mg
Sodium	257.2mg
Carbohydrates	50.8g
Protein	4.7g

Ingredients

2 eggs
3/4 C. dark brown sugar, packed
3/4 C. light molasses
3/4 C. butter, melted
2 1/2 C. all-purpose flour
2 tsps ground ginger
1 1/2 tsps ground cinnamon
1/2 tsp ground cloves

1/2 tsp ground nutmeg
1/2 tsp baking soda
1/2 tsp salt
1 C. boiling water
1 C. pecans, chopped

Directions

1. Before you do anything, preheat the oven to 350 F.
2. Get a large mixing bowl: Mix in it the eggs, brown sugar, molasses and melted butter.
3. Add to it the rest of the ingredients and combine them well. Add the boiling water and mix them well.
4. Transfer the mix to a greased cake pan. Cook it in the oven for 36 min.
5. Allow the cake to cool down completely then serve it.
6. Enjoy.

HERBED
Chicken and Cajun Skillet

Prep Time: 20 mins
Total Time: 20 mins

Servings per Recipe: 8
Calories	104.3
Fat	2.6g
Cholesterol	24.6mg
Sodium	179.4mg
Carbohydrates	8.8g
Protein	12.5g

Ingredients

3/4 lb skinless chicken breast, cubes
1/2 lb turkey kielbasa, slices
1 medium onion, chopped
3 garlic cloves, minced
1 tbsp olive oil
1 medium green pepper, chopped
1 medium sweet red pepper, chopped
1 medium yellow pepper, chopped
1 lb fresh mushrooms, sliced
2 medium tomatoes, diced

minced fresh herbs
1 1/2 tsps Cajun seasoning
1/2 tsp salt
1/4 tsp pepper
1 tbsp cornstarch
2 tbsp cold water
cooked spaghetti

Directions

1. Place a large pan over medium heat. Heat the oil in it. Cook in it the chicken, kielbasa, onion and garlic for 5 min.

2. Stir in it the peppers, mushrooms, tomatoes, herbs, Cajun seasoning, salt and pepper. Let them cook for 8 min.

3. Get a small mixing bowl: Whisk in it the cornstarch with water. Stir them into the pan. Cook them until they start boiling.

4. Let them cook for 3 min. Serve your stir fry warm.

5. Enjoy.

Mild Cajun
Eggplant Casserole

Prep Time: 30 mins
Total Time: 2 hr

Servings per Recipe: 6
Calories	936.7
Fat	61.1g
Cholesterol	218.7mg
Sodium	1874.2mg
Carbohydrates	58.3g
Protein	40.6g

Ingredients

1 1/2 C. all-purpose flour
3 large eggs
1 C. milk
4 C. breadcrumbs
1 1/2 large eggplants, sliced
8 tbsp olive oil
2 1/2 C. mild salsa

1/2 lb tasso or 1/2 lb hot capocollo, chopped
1/2 lb andouille sausages or 1/2 lb beef links, chopped
2 C. cheddar cheese, grated
2 C. cheddar cheese, grated

Directions

1. Before you do anything, preheat the oven to 350 F.
2. Get a large mixing bowl: Mix in it eggs with milk.
3. Dust an eggplant slice with flour then coat it with milk mix and roll it in the breadcrumbs. Place it on a lined up baking pan.
4. Repeat the process with the remaining ingredients.
5. Place a large pan over medium heat. Heat in it 2 tbsp of oil. Fry in it the eggplant slices for 4 min on each side.
6. Lay half of the eggplant slices in a greased baking dish. Top it with 1 1/2 of salsa, all the ham and sausage. Sprinkle 1 1/2 C. of cheese over it.
7. Lay the remaining eggplant slices on top then spread the remaining salsa over it followed by the remaining cheese.
8. Place the pan in the oven and let it cook for 46 min. Serve it hot.
9. Enjoy.

CREOLE
Any-Noodles Salad

Prep Time: 20 mins
Total Time: 40 mins

Servings per Recipe: 10
Calories	212.2
Fat	8.9g
Cholesterol	19.1mg
Sodium	633.2mg
Carbohydrates	29.3g
Protein	6.4g

Ingredients

4 oz. chopped black olives
1 cans sliced mushrooms
1/2 red onion, sliced very thin
3 small tomatoes, chopped
1 small bell pepper, sliced
15 oz. artichoke hearts
2 sliced cucumbers

3 stalks celery
8 oz. Italian dressing
Salad Supreme dry seasoning
8 oz. cooked noodles, any
salt and pepper

Directions

1. Prepare the pasta by following the directions on the package. Drain it.

2. Get a large mixing bowl: Toss the pasta with the remaining ingredients. Serve it right way.

3. Enjoy.

White Fish and Creole
Potato Casserole

🥣 Prep Time: 15 mins
🕐 Total Time: 1 hr

Servings per Recipe: 4
Calories	143.1
Fat	1.1g
Cholesterol	38.0mg
Sodium	106.7mg
Carbohydrates	20.6g
Protein	13.5g

Ingredients

2 medium sweet potatoes, sliced
1/2 onion, peeled and sliced thinly
1/2-3/4 lb white fish fillet
1 dash creole seasoning
3-5 garlic cloves, peeled

4 C. spinach, chopped
8 small roma tomatoes, diced

Directions

1. Before you do anything, preheat the oven to 450 F.
2. Grease a Dutch oven with some olive oil. Lay in it onion slices followed by the white fish fillets. Season them with the Cajun seasoning.
3. Top it with potatoes, garlic, onions, and tomatoes. Lay the spinach on top then season them with some salt and pepper.
4. Place the pot in the oven and let them cook for 44 min. Serve your fish casserole warm.
5. Enjoy.

OKRA
Jumbo Stew

Prep Time: 10 mins
Total Time: 30 mins

Servings per Recipe: 4
Calories   932.2
Fat   44.5g
Cholesterol   372.4mg
Sodium   2426.1mg
Carbohydrates   25.7g
Protein   103.2g

Ingredients

2 tbsp vegetable oil
1 lb turkey sausage, sliced
2 lbs chicken tenders, diced
1 medium yellow onion, sliced
3 large garlic cloves, chopped
3 celery ribs, chopped
1 green pepper, thin strips
1 red bell pepper, thin strips
4 sprigs fresh thyme
2 C. chicken stock

1 C. tomato juice
1/4 C. hot sauce
1 lb medium raw shrimp, peeled and deveined
8 oz. frozen okra, defrosted
1/4 C. fresh flat-leaf parsley, chopped
4 scallions, green and white parts, thinly sliced

Directions

1. Place a large pan over medium heat. Heat the oil in it.
2. Cook in it the sausage for 4 min. Push it to one side of the pan. Cook the chicken tenders on the other side with a pinch of salt and pepper for 4 min.
3. Add the onion with garlic, celery, bell peppers, thyme, a pinch of salt and pepper. Mix them all well and let them cook for 6 min.
4. Stir in the stock, tomato sauce, and hot sauce. Cook them until they start boiling.
5. Stir in the shrimp and okra. Put on the lid and let them cook for 6 min. fold the parsley and scallions into the stew then serve it hot.
6. Enjoy.

Smoked
Venison Jerky

🥄 Prep Time: 15 mins
🕐 Total Time: 24 hr 15 mins

Servings per Recipe: 15
Calories   99.2
Fat   4.3g
Cholesterol   48.4mg
Sodium   90.5mg
Carbohydrates   1.1g
Protein   13.2g

Ingredients

2 lbs ground venison
1/4 C. Cajun seasoning
1/4 C. Worcestershire sauce

1/4 C. liquid smoke
1 tbsp black pepper

Directions

1. Get a large mixing bowl: Stir in it all the ingredients. Spread the mix on the dehydrating trays.
2. Dehydrate the jerky for 6 h 20 min on 156 degrees. Serve your jerky right away or store them sealing bags.
3. Enjoy.

...eans

Servings per Recipe: 8

Calories	630 kcal
Fat	24.2 g
Carbohydrates	79.1g
Protein	24 g
Cholesterol	33 mg
Sodium	604 mg

Ingredients

1 lb dry kidney beans
1/4 C. olive oil
1 large onion, chopped
1 green bell pepper, chopped
2 tbsps minced garlic
2 stalks celery, chopped
6 C. water
2 bay leaves
1/2 tsp cayenne pepper

1 tsp dried thyme
1/4 tsp dried sage
1 tbsp dried parsley
1 tsp Cajun seasoning
1 lb andouille sausage, sliced
4 C. water
2 C. long grain white rice

Directions

1. Get a bowl and fill it with water. Leave your beans submerged in the water for at least 8 hrs or throughout the night.
2. For 6 mins fry in olive oil: celery, onions, garlic, and bell peppers.
3. Add 6 C. of water to a saucepan and then transfer your beans to it after rinsing them.
4. Combine in your onions, peppers, and the following: Cajun seasoning, bay leaves, parsley, cayenne, sage, and thyme.
5. Get the mix boiling then set the heat to low and let the mix lightly cook for 2 h 40 m.
6. Now combine in your sausage and let everything continue cooking for 35 more mins.
7. Get a 2nd saucepan and bring some water to a boil. Enter in your rice, place a lid on the pot, and let the rice cook for 22 mins.
8. Enjoy your rice with the beans.

Easy
Chicken Fry

Prep Time: 10 mins
Total Time: 30 mins

Servings per Recipe: 6
Calories	638 kcal
Fat	29.6 g
Carbohydrates	47.9 g
Protein	42.7 g
Cholesterol	177 mg
Sodium	960 mg

Ingredients

1 (3 lb) whole chicken, cut into 6 pieces
2 eggs, beaten
1 (12 fluid oz.) can evaporated milk
2 tsps salt
2 tsps ground black pepper
2 tsps garlic powder

2 tsps onion powder
2 1/2 C. all-purpose flour
1 1/2 C. vegetable oil for frying

Directions

1. Get a bowl mix: milk, onion powder, eggs, garlic powder, pepper, and salt.
2. Get a 2nd bowl and add the flour to it.
3. Coat the chicken first with the wet mix and then the dry flour.
4. Now fry your chicken in hot oil for about 7 to 10 mins per side until it is fully done.
5. Enjoy.

ETOUFFEE

Prep Time: 15 mins
Total Time: 30 mins

Servings per Recipe: 6
Calories	636 kcal
Fat	24.6 g
Carbohydrates	82.7g
Protein	19.4 g
Cholesterol	142 mg
Sodium	601 mg

Ingredients

3 C. long grain white rice
6 C. water
3/4 C. butter
1 large onion, chopped
1 clove garlic, chopped
1/4 C. all-purpose flour
1 lb crawfish tails
2 tbsps canned tomato sauce
1 C. water, or as needed

6 green onions, chopped
salt and pepper to taste
1 1/2 tbsps Cajun seasoning, or to taste

Directions

1. Boil your water in a large pot then add your rice.
2. Place a lid on the pot, set the heat to its lowest level and lightly boil for 22 mins.
3. Stir fry your onions in butter until they are see-through and then add your garlic.
4. Continue stirring for 2 mins then add the flour to the onions and stir for a few more mins.
5. Then add the crawfish, water, and tomato sauce. Get everything simmering and then add your salt, Cajun seasoning, green onions, and pepper.
6. Let everything simmer for about 12 to 15 mins with a low level of heat.
7. Enjoy your fish over the rice.

Shrimp
Bake

Prep Time: 15 mins
Total Time: 40 mins

Servings per Recipe: 4	
Calories	572 kcal
Fat	31.9 g
Carbohydrates	38.5g
Protein	31.8 g
Cholesterol	250 mg
Sodium	1150 mg

Ingredients

1 1/2 C. uncooked instant rice
1 1/2 C. water
1 tsp vegetable oil
1 lb small shrimp, peeled and deveined
2 tbsps butter
1 (4 oz.) can sliced mushrooms, drained

1 (10.75 oz.) can condensed cream of shrimp soup
1 (8 oz.) container sour cream
3/4 C. shredded Cheddar cheese

Directions

1. Coat a casserole dish with oil and then turn on the broiler to low, if possible, before doing anything else.
2. Get a saucepan and boil your water.
3. Then enter your rice into and it and place a lid on the pot.
4. Set the heat to low and let the rice cook for 12 mins. Now shut off the heat.
5. Stir fry your shrimp for 4 mins, in oil, then place them in a bowl.
6. In the same pot add some butter and fry your mushrooms for 3 mins then add in your sour cream and soup.
7. Get the soup hot but avoid boiling it.
8. Now add the shrimp back to the pan and heat it up.
9. Put everything in your casserole dish including the rice.
10. Garnish the casserole with some cheese and cook everything under the broiler for 5 mins.
11. Enjoy.

NEW ORLEANS STYLE
Pancakes

Prep Time: 10 mins
Total Time: 45 mins

Servings per Recipe: 8

Calories	215 kcal
Fat	8.2 g
Carbohydrates	29.2g
Protein	6.2 g
Cholesterol	65 mg
Sodium	549 mg

Ingredients

3/4 lb sweet potatoes
1 1/2 C. all-purpose flour
3 1/2 tsps baking powder
1 tsp salt
1/2 tsp ground nutmeg

2 eggs, beaten
1 1/2 C. milk
1/4 C. butter, melted

Directions

1. For 17 mins boil your sweet potatoes in water.
2. Dump these potatoes in a bowl of cold water immediately after boiling them. Then remove all the skins, chunk them, and mash them.
3. Get a bowl, sift: nutmeg, flour, salt, and baking powder.
4. Get a 2nd bowl, combine: butter, potatoes, milk, and eggs.
5. Heat up a frying pan or a griddle that has been oiled or coated with nonstick spray.
6. Now combine both bowls to form a batter.
7. Fry tbsps of this mixture until you find one side begins to form bubbles, then flip the pancake and cook it for the same amount of time.
8. The cooking time is very dependent upon the heat of stove.
9. Enjoy.

Gumbo

Prep Time: 20 mins
Total Time: 3 hrs 55 mins

Servings per Recipe: 10
Calories	437 kcal
Fat	32.2 g
Carbohydrates	14.5g
Protein	21.4 g
Cholesterol	67 mg
Sodium	873 mg

Ingredients

1 (3 lb) whole chicken
1/2 C. all-purpose flour
1/2 C. vegetable oil
1 (10 oz.) package frozen chopped onions
1 (10 oz.) package frozen green bell peppers
5 stalks celery, finely chopped
1 tbsp Cajun seasoning (such as Tony Chachere's), or to taste

2 whole bay leaves
1 (28 oz.) can diced tomatoes
1 lb fully-cooked smoked beef sausage (such as Hillshire Farm(R)), sliced
1 (10 oz.) package frozen sliced okra
salt and black pepper to taste

Directions

1. Boil your water and salt, then simmer your chicken in it for 1 hour until fully cooked.
2. Take the chicken out from the water and cut it in half to cool faster.
3. Keep the water the chicken was cooked in.
4. Once the chicken is no longer hot take off the meat from the bones.
5. Now get a big pan and mix: veggie oil and flour together to form a roux.
6. Make this roux with a low level of heat and constantly stir it for about 22 mins until it becomes brown.
7. Once it is brown add in: bay leaves, onions, Cajun seasoning, celery and bell peppers.
8. Again with a low heat let the veggies simmer for 40 mins.
9. Now add the chicken broth (the boiled water), sausage, and diced tomatoes.
10. Let the contents simmer for 1 more hour.
11. Now add in your meat from the chicken and your okra and let everything simmer for 50 more mins.
12. Enjoy your gumbo.

Louisiana

Prep Time: 15 mins
Total Time: 2 hrs 45 mins

Servings per Recipe: 8

Calories	531 kcal
Fat	22.6 g
Carbohydrates	57g
Protein	23.9 g
Cholesterol	81 mg
Sodium	616 mg

Ingredients

2 tbsps all-purpose flour
1 tsp salt
1/2 tsp celery salt
1/4 tsp garlic salt
1/4 tsp black pepper
1/2 tsp ground ginger
3 lbs chuck roast, cut into 2-inch pieces
2 tbsps bacon drippings
1 (14.5 oz.) can diced tomatoes

3 medium onions, chopped
1/3 C. red wine vinegar
1/2 C. molasses
1/2 C. water
6 carrots, chopped
1/2 C. raisins
4 C. cooked rice

Directions

1. Get a bowl, mix evenly: ground ginger, flour, black pepper, garlic salt, regular salt, and celery salt.
2. Coat your meat with this seasoning.
3. Stir fry this meat in bacon fat until all sides are nice and brown.
4. Now combine in: water, diced tomatoes, molasses, onions, and vinegar. Place a lid on your pot and let the contents lightly boil with a low heat for 2 hrs.
5. Now finally add in your raisins and carrots and simmer for 35 more mins.
6. Enjoy with jasmine or your favorite rice.

Sweet Banana
Stir Fry

Prep Time: 5 mins
Total Time: 20 mins

Servings per Recipe: 4
Calories	534 kcal
Fat	23.8 g
Carbohydrates	73.2g
Protein	4.6 g
Cholesterol	60 mg
Sodium	146 mg

Ingredients

1/4 C. butter
2/3 C. dark brown sugar
3 1/2 tbsps rum
1 1/2 tsps vanilla extract
1/2 tsp ground cinnamon
3 bananas, peeled and sliced lengthwise
and crosswise

1/4 C. coarsely chopped walnuts
1 pint vanilla ice cream

Directions

1. Stir fry the following in butter: cinnamon, sugar, vanilla, and rum.
2. Once the mix is bubbly add your nuts and bananas.
3. Let the contents simmer for 3 mins.
4. Enjoy with ice cream.

STREET
ball Stew

Prep Time: 45 mins

Total Time: 1 hr 45 mins

Servings per Recipe: 6

Calories	765.9
Fat	55.7g
Cholesterol	167.7mg
Sodium	208.4mg
Carbohydrates	32.3g
Protein	33.3g

Ingredients

3/4 C. vegetable oil
1 C. all-purpose flour
3 C. onions, finely chopped
1 1/2 C. bell peppers, finely chopped
1 C. celery, finely chopped
water or beef broth
4 garlic cloves, minced
2 lbs ground chuck
2 large eggs

1/4 C. milk
1 tbsp Worcestershire sauce
1/2 C. fresh parsley, chopped
1/3 C. plain breadcrumbs
salt and cayenne pepper
1/4 C. green onion, chopped

Directions

1. Place a large pot over medium heat. Heat the oil in it. Mix the flour into it and cook it until it becomes golden brown.
2. Mix in it 2 C. of the chopped onion, 1 C. of the bell pepper and 1/2 C. of the celery. Cook them for 5 to 6 min.
3. Pour enough broth or water in the pot to fill 2/3 of it. Cook the soup until it starts boiling. Lower the heat and let it cook.
4. Get a large mixing bowl: Mix in it the ground chuck, remaining onions, bell pepper, and celery, 2 cloves of the minced garlic and eggs.
5. Add the milk with worcestershire sauce, 1/4 C. of the parsley, bread crumbs, and salt and cayenne pepper then mix them well.
6. Shape the mix into bite size meatballs. Lower the meatballs into the pot and let them cook for 22 min without stirring them.
7. Add the cayenne pepper, rest of the garlic, parsley, green onion and a pinch of salt. Cook the stew for an extra 6 min. Serve your stew hot with some rice.
8. Enjoy.

Cajun
Vanilla Pie

🥣 Prep Time: 25 mins
🕐 Total Time: 1 hr 55 mins

Servings per Recipe: 8
Calories   420.9
Fat   14.7g
Cholesterol   89.5mg
Sodium   337.9mg
Carbohydrates   69.7g
Protein   4.6g

Ingredients

3 medium sweet potatoes, boiled and mashed
1/4 C. brown sugar
2 tbsp sugar
1 tbsp butter
1 tbsp pure vanilla extract
1 large egg
1 tbsp heavy cream
1/4 tsp ground cinnamon
1 pinch nutmeg
1 pinch ground allspice
1 9" unbaked pie shell

1/2 C. chopped pecans
3/4 C. granulated sugar
2 large eggs
3/4 C. dark corn syrup
1 tbsp butter, melted
1/2 tsp salt
ground cinnamon
2 tsps pure vanilla extract
whipped cream

Directions

1. Before you do anything, preheat the oven to 300 F.
2. Get a large mixing bowl: Beat in it the sweet potatoes, both sugars, butter, vanilla, egg, cinnamon, nutmeg, and allspice until they become smooth.
3. Spoon the mix into the pie crust. Garnish it with the pecans.
4. Get a mixing bowl: Mix in it the granulated sugar, eggs, corn syrup, melted butter, salt, cinnamon and vanilla.
5. Sprinkle the mix over the pecan layer. Place the pie in the oven and let it cook for 1 h 32 min.
6. Allow the pie to cool down completely then serve it with your favorite toppings.
7. Enjoy.

BLACKENED POTATO
Crusted Shrimp

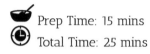

Prep Time: 15 mins
Total Time: 25 mins

Servings per Recipe: 4
Calories   142.8
Fat   7.9g
Cholesterol   143.0mg
Sodium   642.5mg
Carbohydrates   1.7g
Protein   15.5g

Ingredients

1 lb jumbo shrimp, shelled and deveined
1 tsp blackening seasoning
2 C. frozen Hash Browns

2 tbsp vegetable oil
1 small lemon

Directions

1. Get a large mixing bowl: Toss in it the shrimp with Cajun blackening seasoning.
2. Place a large pan over medium heat. Heat the oil in it. Press the potato hash into the shrimp then cook them in the hot oil for 4 to 5 min on each side.
3. Squeeze over them some fresh lemon juice.
4. Enjoy.

French Quarter
Green Beans

Prep Time: 30 mins
Total Time: 1 hr 30 mins

Servings per Recipe: 6
Calories   438.8
Fat   29.9g
Cholesterol   85.7mg
Sodium   837.1mg
Carbohydrates   27.9g
Protein   18.1g

Ingredients

4 slices thick-sliced turkey bacon, cut into pieces
2 small onions, chopped
2 garlic cloves
3 lbs green beans
1/4 C. butter
1 pinch of grated nutmeg
1/2 C. all-purpose flour

1/2 C. heavy cream
1 1/2 C. grated white cheddar cheese
4 C. chicken broth
salt and pepper
2 (6 oz.) cans fried onions

Directions

1. Before you do anything, preheat the oven to 350 F.
2. Place a dutch oven over medium heat. Cook in it the bacon for 5 min. Stir into it the onion and cook them for 7 min. Stir in the garlic and cook them for 2 min. Place it aside.
3. Stir in the green beans with enough broth or water to cover it in a large saucepan.
4. Lower the heat put on the lid. Let the mix cook for 30 min. Drain the beans and reserve the cooking liquid.
5. Place a large pan over medium heat. Heat in it the butter until it melts. Sauté in it the rest of the onion with salt and nutmeg. Place it aside.
6. Cook them for 7 min. Mix in the flour followed by the cream and the reserved bean cooking liquid. Cook it for 6 min until it mixture becomes thick.
7. Add the cheese and green beans and cook them for few minutes until the cheese melts.
8. Pour the mix into a glass casserole dish. Place it in the oven and let it cook for 26 min. Spread the onion and bacon mix on top.
9. Bake it for an extra 14 min. Serve it hot.
10. Enjoy.

HOUMA
Potato Pots

Prep Time: 20 mins
Total Time: 1 hr 50 mins

Servings per Recipe: 2

Calories	642.4
Fat	32.5g
Cholesterol	375.2mg
Sodium	1689.0mg
Carbohydrates	37.3g
Protein	49.4g

Ingredients

1 lb jumbo shrimp, deveined
2 large baking potatoes
1 C. guacamole
3 tbsp Cajun seasoning
2 tbsp minced garlic

1/2 C. sour cream
1 C. shredded cheddar cheese

Directions

1. Before you do anything, preheat the grill.
2. Place each potato in the middle of piece of foil and wrap it around it. Place it on the grill and let them cook until they become slightly soft.
3. Toss the shrimp with Cajun seasoning and garlic in a shallow roasting pan. Place the pan over the grill on the indirect side of it.
4. Let the shrimp cook for 12 min. Flip it and let cook for another 12 min.
5. Once the shrimp and potato are done place them aside to lose heat for a while.
6. Discard the foil sheets and slice them in half. Spoon some of the potato flesh to leave 1/4 of it only.
7. Place 4 shrimp aside. Chop the remaining shrimp and place it in the potato shells followed by the cheese.
8. Place each one of them in a foil packet. Place them over the grill and let them cook for an extra 12 min.
9. Place the 4 shrimps in a small foil packet and grill them for 6 min.
10. Once the time is up, top the shrimp layer with guacamole and sour cream. Garnish them with the whole remaining 4 shrimps. Serve them right away.
11. Enjoy.

Baked Sole
with Cauliflower
Salad

Prep Time: 10 mins
Total Time: 40 mins

Servings per Recipe: 2
Calories   744.6
Fat   14.0g
Cholesterol   328.2mg
Sodium   1111.4mg
Carbohydrates   22.8g
Protein   129.0g

Ingredients

8 sole fillets
3 C. French style green beans
3 C. cauliflower, florettes
1 tbsp butter
1/8 C. lemon juice
1 green onion

salt
pepper
cajun seasoning

Directions

1. Before you do anything, preheat the oven to 350 F.
2. Place the sole fillets on a greased baking pan. Drizzle over them the fresh lemon juice followed by the Cajun seasoning.
3. Place the sole sheet in the oven and let it coo for 32 min.
4. Place the cauliflower in a heatproof bowl. Cook it in the microwave for 9 min.
5. Get a heatproof bowl: Stir in it the green beans with green onion. Cook them in the microwave for 9 min.
6. Drain the coked veggies. Add to them the butter with a pinch of salt and pepper. Toss them to coat.
7. Serve your baked sole with the veggies salad.
8. Enjoy.

ntry Hens

Prep Time: 10 mins
Total Time: 24 hrs 10 mins

Servings per Recipe: 4
Calories   1602.6
Fat   107.1g
Cholesterol   756.2mg
Sodium   389.7mg
Carbohydrates   20.1g
Protein   129.3g

Ingredients

4 oz. hot smoked sausage, chopped
1/2 C. long grain white rice
1 cans diced tomatoes
1/2 C. sliced green onion
1/4 C. chopped green bell pepper
1 garlic clove, minced

1/4 tsp dried thyme leaves
4 Cornish hens
1 tbsp butter, melted

Directions

1. Place a pot over medium heat. Cook in it the sausages for 8 min. Add the rice and let them cook for 3 min.

2. Stir in the tomatoes, onions, pepper, garlic and thyme. Cook them until they start boiling. Put on the lid and let them cook for 22 min.

3. Spoon the mix into the cavity of the hens. Place them in a greased roasting pan and coat them with butter, a pinch of salt and pepper.

4. Place them in the oven and let them cook for 60 min. Allow them to rest for 5 min then serve them warm.

5. Enjoy.

Lake Charles
Avocado Glazed Kabobs

🥄 Prep Time: 15 mins
🕐 Total Time: 25 mins

Servings per Recipe: 2
Calories	525.3
Fat	47.7g
Cholesterol	85.6mg
Sodium	482.4mg
Carbohydrates	18.0g
Protein	11.7g

Ingredients

20 large uncooked prawns, peeled and deveined
2 tbsp Cajun seasoning
2 tsps ground cumin
1 tsp dried oregano
2 garlic cloves, crushed
50 ml olive oil
1 large avocado

2 tbsp sour cream
2 tbsp mayonnaise
1 tsp Tabasco sauce
1/2 tsp garlic powder
1 tbsp fresh coriander, chopped
1 tbsp lemon juice

Directions

1. Get a large mixing bowl: Stir in it the prawns with Cajun seasoning, oregano, cumin, garlic, olive oil, a pinch of salt and pepper.
2. Place the mix in the fridge to sit for at least 30 min.
3. Before you do anything, preheat the grill and grease it.
4. Drain the prawns and thread them into skewers. Place them on the grill and cook them for 4 to 5 min on each side.
5. Get a blender: Place in it all the avocado sauce ingredients. Blend them smooth.
6. Serve your skewers warm with the avocado sauce.
7. Enjoy.

CAJUN
Pilaf

Prep Time: 10 mins
Total Time: 30 mins

Servings per Recipe: 2
Calories	530.8
Fat	5.9 g
Cholesterol	127.8mg
Sodium	514.2mg
Carbohydrates	70.5g
Protein	45.0g

Ingredients

cooking spray
1 small brown onion, chopped
2 celery ribs, chopped
2 garlic cloves, crushed
1/4 tsp ground cinnamon
2 cloves
1/4 tsp ground turmeric
3/4 C. long-grain white rice

2 C. chicken stock
1/4 C. flat leaf parsley, chopped
360 g white fish fillets
2 tsps Cajun seasoning

Directions

1. Place a pot over medium heat. Heat the oil in it. Add the onion, celery and garlic. Let them cook for 6 min.
2. Stir in the seasonings and cook them for 1 min. Stir in the rice and cook them for an extra 2 min.
3. Pour in the broth and cook them until they start boiling. Lower the heat and put on the lid. Cook the pilaf for 22 min.
4. Fold the parsley into te pilaf.
5. Place a large pan over medium heat. Heat a splash of oil in it.
6. Season the fish fillets with Cajun spice, a pinch of salt and pepper. Cook them in the hot oil for 4 to 6 min on each side.
7. Serve your fish fillets warm with the pilaf.
8. Enjoy.

Creole Vegetarian Casserole

Prep Time: 15 mins
Total Time: 17 mins

Servings per Recipe: 4
Calories   173.4
Fat   3.5g
Cholesterol   57.1mg
Sodium   332.9mg
Carbohydrates   30.2g
Protein   8.0g

Ingredients

1/2 tsp salt
3/4 tsp sweet paprika
1/4-1/2 tsp cayenne pepper, to taste
1/2 tsp ground black pepper
1/4 tsp dried thyme leaves
1 1/2 lbs summer squash or 1 1/2 lbs zucchini, cut in rounds
1/2 C. whole wheat flour

1/2 C. cornmeal
1/2 C. milk
1 egg
safflower oil

Directions

1. Get a mixing bowl: Mix in it the salt, spices, and thyme.
2. Get a large mixing bowl: Toss in it the squash with 1 tsp of the spice mix.
3. Get a mixing bowl: Stir in it the flour with half of the remaining spice mix.
4. Get a mixing bowl: Stir in it the cornmeal with the remaining half of the spice mix.
5. Get a mixing bowl: Whisk in it the egg with milk.
6. Dust the squash slices with the flour mix then dip them in the milk mix followed by the cornmeal mix.
7. Place a large pan over medium heat. Heat in it 1 inch of oil. Cook in it the squash slices for 3 min until they become golden brown.
8. Serve your squash fries with your favorite sauce.
9. Enjoy.

11-INGREDIENT
Jambalaya

Prep Time: 30 mins
Total Time: 1 hr 15 mins

Servings per Recipe: 4
Calories	439.1
Fat	17.1g
Cholesterol	32.3mg
Sodium	1526.0mg
Carbohydrates	55.3g
Protein	17.9g

Ingredients

rotisserie chicken, chopped
1/2 lb Andouille sausage, sliced
1 medium onion, of choice chopped
1 medium green bell pepper, chopped
1 tbsp minced garlic
2 cans Rotel Tomatoes
1 C. chicken broth
2 C. penne pasta, uncooked

1 tbsp italian seasoning
1 tsp Cajun seasoning
2 stalks green onions, sliced

Directions

1. Place a large pot over medium heat. Cook in it the sausages for 8 min. Drain it and place it aside.
2. Stir the bell pepper with onion into the same pan and cook them for 5 min. Stir in the garlic and cook them for 2 min.
3. Add the chicken with cooked sausage to the pan with the remaining ingredients. Cook them until they start boiling.
4. Lower the heat and put on the lid. Cook the stew for 26 min. serve your stew warm.
5. Enjoy.

Louisianan
Trail Mix

🥣 Prep Time: 5 mins
🕐 Total Time: 20 mins

Servings per Recipe: 1
Calories	734.4
Fat	32.5g
Cholesterol	0.0mg
Sodium	362.4mg
Carbohydrates	101.9g
Protein	17.8g

Ingredients

22 oz. boxes wheat squares
18.5 oz. boxes oat o's cereal
3.5 oz packages pretzel sticks
1 box cheddar cheese crackers
1 C. roasted peanuts
1/2 C. canola oil

2 tbsp hot sauce
1/4 C. Cajun seasoning
1/4 C. garlic powder

Directions

1. Before you do anything, preheat the oven to 325 F.
2. Mix the wheat squares with cereal, pretzel sticks, cheese crackers and peanuts in a shallow baking pan.
3. Get a mixing bowl: Mix in it the oil with Cajun seasoning, garlic powder, and hot sauce. Add the mix to the cereal mix and toss them to coat.
4. Place the pan in the middle of the oven and let it cook for 16 min.
5. Allow your trail road mix to lose heat completely then serve it.
6. Enjoy.

BATON ROUGE
Bisque

Prep Time: 20 mins
Total Time: 50 mins

Servings per Recipe: 8
Calories	431.7
Fat	31.5g
Cholesterol	145.7mg
Sodium	363.7mg
Carbohydrates	23.2g
Protein	16.7g

Ingredients

3 tbsp butter
3 tbsp all-purpose flour
1 tbsp vegetable oil
1 large onion, chopped
1 tbsp minced garlic
1 large celery, minced
cajun seasoning
1 C. chicken broth
1 1/2 C. frozen corn kernels
1 bay leaf
2 C. milk
2 C. heavy cream
1 tsp liquid shrimp and crab boil seasoning
1 lb fresh lump crabmeat
1/4 C. chopped green onion
1/2 tsp Worcestershire sauce
salt and pepper
chopped green onion

Directions

1. Place a large heavy saucepan over medium heat.
2. Heat in it the butter. Add to it the flour and mix it well. Let it cook for 6 min while mixing it all the time. Turn off the heat.
3. Place a large pot over medium heat. Heat the oil in it. Sauté in it the onion, garlic, and celery for 2 min.
4. Stir in the Cajun seasoning with broth, corn, and bay leaf. Cook it until it starts simmering. Add the milk, cream, and liquid crab boil seasoning.
5. Bring the soup to a simmer then lower the heat and let it cook for 8 min. add the flour and butter mix gradually to the soup wile mixing all the time.
6. Let the soup cook for 10 min over low heat until it becomes thick. Add the crabmeat, green onions, and Worcestershire sauce.
7. Cook the soup for an extra 7 min. Adjust the seasoning of the chowder then serve it hot.
8. Enjoy..

Cajun
Aoli

🥣 Prep Time: 10 mins
🕐 Total Time: 10 mins

Servings per Recipe: 1
Calories   534.1
Fat   39.6g
Cholesterol   33.0mg
Sodium   931.3mg
Carbohydrates   38.9g
Protein   8.4g

Ingredients

1/2 C. mayonnaise
1/2 C. nonfat plain yogurt
1/2 tsp dried oregano
1/4 tsp garlic salt

1/4 tsp ground cumin
1/8 tsp cayenne pepper
1/8 tsp black pepper

Directions

1. Get a small mixing bowl: Whisk in it all the ingredients. Place the mayonnaise in the fridge until ready to serve.

2. Enjoy.

...AYA

Servings per Recipe: 12

Calories	235 kcal
Fat	13.6 g
Carbohydrates	6.1g
Protein	20.2 g
Cholesterol	99 mg
Sodium	688 mg

Ingredients

1 lb skinless, boneless chicken breast
halves - cut into 1 inch cubes
1 lb andouille sausage, sliced
1 (28 oz.) can diced tomatoes with juice
1 large onion, chopped
1 large green bell pepper, chopped
1 C. chopped celery
1 C. chicken broth
2 tsps dried oregano

2 tsps dried parsley
2 tsps Cajun seasoning
1 tsp cayenne pepper
1/2 tsp dried thyme
1 lb frozen cooked shrimp without tails

Directions

1. Cook the following on low for 8 hours in your slow cooker: thyme, chicken, cayenne, sausage, Cajun seasoning, tomatoes and juice, parsley, onions, oregano, bell peppers, broth, and celery.

2. Enjoy with rice.

Gumbo II

Prep Time: 1 hr
Total Time: 2 hrs

Servings per Recipe: 10
Calories	419 kcal
Fat	28.7 g
Carbohydrates	17.3g
Protein	20.5 g
Cholesterol	99 mg
Sodium	900 mg

Ingredients

1 tbsp olive oil
1 C. skinless, boneless chicken breast halves - chopped
1/2 lb pork sausage links, thinly sliced
1 C. olive oil
1 C. all-purpose flour
2 tbsps minced garlic
3 quarts chicken broth
1 (12 fluid oz.) can or bottle beer
6 stalks celery, diced

4 roma (plum) tomatoes, diced
1 sweet onion, sliced
1 (10 oz.) can diced tomatoes with green chili peppers, with liquid
2 tbsps chopped fresh red chili peppers
1 bunch fresh parsley, chopped
1/4 C. Cajun seasoning
1 lb shrimp, peeled and deveined

Directions

1. Stir fry your chicken in hot oil until fully done. Then add in your sausage and continue to stir fry until it is done as well.
2. Place the contents in a bowl.
3. In the same pan or a new one make a roux with flour and olive oil.
4. Once it is brown add your garlic and stir fry the mix for 2 mins.
5. Combine the following with your roux while stirring: beer, and broth.
6. Get the roux simmering and then add: Cajun seasoning, celery, parsley, tomatoes, red chili peppers, sweet onions, diced tomatoes.
7. Let your roux lightly boil with a covering for 45 mins with low heat.
8. Stir the roux every 5 to 7 mins.
9. Then combine in your sausage and chicken and simmer for 25 more mins.
10. Enjoy.

AYA

Prep Time: 20 mins
Total Time: 1 hr 5 mins

Servings per Recipe: 6	
Calories	465 kcal
Fat	19.8 g
Carbohydrates	42.4g
Protein	28.1 g
Cholesterol	73 mg
Sodium	1633 mg

Ingredients

2 tbsps peanut oil, divided
1 tbsp Cajun seasoning
10 oz. andouille sausage, sliced into rounds
1 lb boneless skinless chicken breasts, cut into 1 inch pieces
1 onion, diced
1 small green bell pepper, diced
2 stalks celery, diced
3 cloves garlic, minced
1 (16 oz.) can crushed Italian tomatoes

1/2 tsp red pepper flakes
1/2 tsp ground black pepper
1 tsp salt
1/2 tsp hot pepper sauce
2 tsps Worcestershire sauce
1 tsp file powder
1 1/4 C. uncooked white rice
2 1/2 C. chicken broth

Directions

1. Get a bowl, mix: chicken and sausage with Cajun seasoning.
2. Then fry your seasoned meats in 2 tbsps of peanut oil in a Dutch oven until fully browned.
3. Now put the meats in a 2nd bowl.
4. Add to the same pot: garlic, onions, celery, and bell peppers.
5. Stir the contents fry until everything is soft then add: hot sauce, file powder, red pepper, salt, Worcestershire, black pepper, and crushed tomatoes.
6. Cook the mix for 5 mins then add your meats and cook everything for 13 more mins.
7. Add the broth and the rice.
8. Get everything boiling, set the heat to low, and let the contents simmer for 30 mins until all the liquid has evaporated.
9. Enjoy.

Jambalaya III

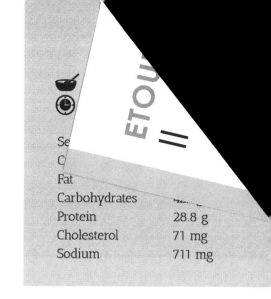

Se...	
C...	
Fat	
Carbohydrates	
Protein	28.8 g
Cholesterol	71 mg
Sodium	711 mg

Ingredients

8 skinless, boneless chicken breast halves - diced
6 C. chicken broth
3 C. long grain white rice
1 lb smoked sausage, sliced
1/4 C. vegetable oil
1 green bell pepper, seeded and chopped
1 small onion, finely chopped
4 carrots, thinly sliced
2 stalks celery, thinly sliced

1 (8 oz.) can mushroom pieces, drained
1/4 tsp cayenne pepper, or to taste
salt and pepper to taste

Directions

1. Stir fry your onions until tender, in oil, in a big pot.
2. Then combine in your chicken and stir fry it until the chicken is browned evenly.
3. Combine in the following with your chicken and onions: sausage, carrots, bell pepper, mushrooms, and celery.
4. Cook this mix for 2 mins while stirring.
5. Now add your broth and get it boiling.
6. Once everything is boiling pour in your pepper, cayenne, salt, and rice.
7. Place a lid on the pot, set the heat to a low level, and let the rice simmer for 22 mins.
8. At this point all the liquid should have evaporated (if not continue simmering).
9. Enjoy.

FFE

 Prep Time: 20 mins

Total Time: 1 hr 10 mins

Servings per Recipe: 6

Calories	264 kcal
Fat	14 g
Carbohydrates	9 g
Protein	24.9 g
Cholesterol	196 mg
Sodium	956 mg

Ingredients

1/3 C. vegetable oil
1/4 C. all-purpose flour
1 small green bell pepper, diced
1 medium onion, chopped
2 cloves garlic, minced
2 stalks celery, diced
2 fresh tomatoes, chopped
2 tbsps Louisiana-style hot sauce
1/3 tsp ground cayenne pepper
(optional)

2 tbsps seafood seasoning
1/2 tsp ground black pepper
1 C. fish stock
1 lb crawfish tails
1 lb medium shrimp - peeled and deveined

Directions

1. Stir fry flour in a pan for 15 to 22 mins until its color becomes brown.
2. Now add your bell peppers, onions, celery, and garlic.
3. Cook this for 7 mins until tender.
4. Now add the seafood seasoning, fish stock, and tomatoes.
5. Set your heat to the lowest level and let the contents lightly boil for 22 mins.
6. Stir the mix every 3 mins.
7. Finally add in some cayenne and hot sauce and finally your shrimp and crawfish.
8. Let the fish simmer in the sauce 13 mins.
9. Enjoy.

Creole
Angel Hair

🥣 Prep Time: 10 mins

🕐 Total Time: 20 mins

Servings per Recipe: 4

Calories	483 kcal
Fat	17.6 g
Carbohydrates	46g
Protein	34.4 g
Cholesterol	213 mg
Sodium	1271 mg

Ingredients

1 (8 oz.) package angel hair pasta
1/4 C. butter
1 lb shrimp, peeled and deveined
1 clove garlic, minced
1/4 C. all-purpose flour
2 tbsps Cajun seasoning

2 C. milk
1/4 tsp salt
1 tbsp lemon juice

Directions

1. Boil your pasta in water and salt for 7 mins.
2. Stir fry your shrimp for 3 mins in melted butter.
3. Then add in your garlic and cook everything for 3 more mins.
4. Take everything out of the pan and add in the Cajun seasoning and flour.
5. Stir the contents while heating for 7 mins.
6. Slowly add the milk and keep heating it until everything becomes thick.
7. Once your seasoned milk is thick shut off the heat and add in your shrimp and garlic.
8. Add your preferred amount of salt and also some lemon juice, but add the lemon juice first.
9. Ladle Cajun sauce over pasta and enjoy.

NORTHEAST LOUISIANA
Style Cajun Wings

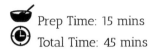

Prep Time: 15 mins
Total Time: 45 mins

Servings per Recipe: 12
Calories	356 kcal
Fat	22.7 g
Carbohydrates	23.9g
Protein	15.6 g
Cholesterol	78 mg
Sodium	896 mg

Ingredients

6 lbs chicken wings, separated at joints,
tips discarded
1 1/2 C. Louisiana-style hot sauce
3/4 C. butter
1 C. honey
1 pinch garlic salt
1 pinch ground black pepper

1 tsp cayenne pepper, or to taste
1 tsp red pepper flakes

Directions

1. You will need a grill for this recipe. So heat yours up after oiling the grate.
2. Cook the chicken on the grill for 10 mins per side until fully done.
3. Then place the chicken in a saucepan.
4. In a 2nd saucepan boil the following for 12 mins: cayenne, hot sauce, black pepper, butter, garlic salt, and honey.
5. Cover your wings in this wet sauce and finally sprinkle on the pepper flakes.
6. Enjoy.
7.
8. NOTE: Instead of using a grill, which is preferred you can fry then, bake these wings for a good taste as well. Fry the chicken first, then coat it with the sauce by tossing the wings in a bowl. Then bake them for a bit in the oven until crispy.

Muffuletta
(Louisiana Sandwhich)

Prep Time: 40 mins
Total Time: 1 d 40 mins

Servings per Recipe: 8
Calories	987 kcal
Fat	62.8 g
Carbohydrates	63.2g
Protein	41.4 g
Cholesterol	97 mg
Sodium	3465 mg

Ingredients

1 C. pimento-stuffed green olives, crushed
1/2 C. drained kalamata olives, crushed
2 cloves garlic, minced
1/4 C. roughly chopped pickled cauliflower florets
2 tbsps drained capers
1 tbsp chopped celery
1 tbsp chopped carrot
1/2 C. pepperoncini, drained
1/4 C. marinated cocktail onions
1/2 tsp celery seed
1 tsp dried oregano

1 tsp dried basil
3/4 tsp ground black pepper
1/4 C. red wine vinegar
1/2 C. olive oil
1/4 C. canola oil
2 (1 lb) loaves Italian bread
8 oz. thinly sliced Genoa salami
8 oz. thinly sliced cooked ham
8 oz. sliced mortadella
8 oz. sliced mozzarella cheese
8 oz. sliced provolone cheese

Directions

1. Get a bowl, combine: all oils, all your olives, vinegar, garlic, black pepper, cauliflower, basil, capers, oregano, celery, celery seed, carrot, pepperoncini, and cocktail onions.
2. Let the salad sit covered in the fridge for at least 6 to 8 hours.
3. Dice your bread into two pieces horizontally.
4. Remove some the insides of the bread to make more space.
5. Top each piece with some salad.
6. On the bottom part of your bread layer: cheese, salami, mortadella, and ham.
7. Form your sandwich and cut it up into serving pieces.
8. Chill the sandwiches before serving for 2 hours in the fridge.
9. Enjoy.

SAINT CLAUDE
Quiche

🥣 Prep Time: 20 mins
🕐 Total Time: 50 mins

Servings per Recipe: 4

Calories	329.9
Fat	12.1g
Cholesterol	73.9mg
Sodium	949.7mg
Carbohydrates	34.6g
Protein	19.3g

Ingredients

2 C. cooked white rice
1 tsp garlic powder
1 tsp onion powder
1/2 tsp salt
1 large egg, lightly beaten
cooking spray
1 oz. cheddar cheese, shredded
1/2 C. onion, diced
1/2 C. celery, diced
1/2 C. red bell pepper, diced
1 tsp garlic, minced

3 oz. Andouille sausages
3/4 C. egg substitute
2 large egg whites, lightly beaten
1/4 C. plain yogurt
1/4 tsp salt
1/4 tsp hot pepper sauce
1 oz. cheddar cheese

Directions

1. Before you do anything, preheat the oven to 375 F.
2. Get a large mixing bowl: Mix in it the white rice with garlic powder, onion powder, salt and beaten egg.
3. Pour the mix into a greased baking glass dish. Top it with 1/4 C. of cheese.
4. Place a large pan over medium heat. Heat a splash of oil in it. Cook in it the onion with celery, bell pepper, garlic and sausage. Cook them for 6 min.
5. Spread the mix over the rice layer.
6. Get a mixing bowl: Whisk in it the egg substitute with egg whites, yogurt, salt and hot pepper sauce. Spread the mix over the veggies layer.
7. Sprinkle the remaining cheese on top. Place the casserole in the oven and let it cook for 35 min. Serve it warm.
8. Enjoy.

Chicken Cutlets
Creole

🥣 Prep Time: 15 mins
🕐 Total Time: 30 mins

Servings per Recipe: 5
Calories   322.2
Fat   13.6g
Cholesterol   59.6mg
Sodium   496.5mg
Carbohydrates   26.4g
Protein   22.8g

Ingredients

10 oz. boneless skinless chicken breasts, baked and cut into pieces
1 C. cheddar cheese, shredded and divided
1/2 C. onion, finely chopped
1/2 C. green pepper, diced
1/4 C. mayonnaise
3/4 tsp Cajun seasoning

1/2 tsp minced garlic
10 slices Italian bread, 1/2-inch thick slices
2 plum tomatoes, sliced

Directions

1. Before you do anything, preheat the oven to 375 F.
2. Get a mixing bowl: Mix in it the chicken with 1/2 C. cheese, onion, green pepper, mayonnaise, Cajun seasoning and garlic.
3. Place the bread slices on a lined up baking sheet. Spoon the chicken mix over them then top them with the tomato slices and the remaining cheese.
4. Place the tray in the oven and cook them for 11 min. Serve your chicken bites warm.
5. Enjoy.

AUNTIES
Cajun Pies

Prep Time: 2 hrs
Total Time: 3 hrs

Servings per Recipe: 15
Calories   354.9
Fat   17.3g
Cholesterol   44.7mg
Sodium   1004.1mg
Carbohydrates   42.0g
Protein   7.5g

Ingredients

5 lbs ground meat
3 tsp salt
1 tsp fresh black pepper
2 tsp chili powder
1 tsp red pepper flakes
2 onions
1 garlic clove, crushed
1 bell pepper, chopped
4 stalks celery, chopped

6 C. all-purpose flour
3 eggs
3 tsp salt
1 1/2 C. whole milk
1 1/2 tsp baking powder
1 C. shortening
1 1/2 tbsp shortening

Directions

1. Place a large pan over medium heat. Cook in it the beef for 8 min. Add to it the remaining filling ingredients.

2. Cook them for 5 min while stirring them often to make the filling. Place it aside to cool down. Get a large mixing bowl: Whisk in it the milk with eggs.

3. Get another mixing bowl: Mix in it the flour with salt, and baking powder. Add the milk mix and combine them well. Mix in the shortening. Place the dough on a lightly floured surface. Use a rolling pin to flatten.

4. Use a cookie cutter to cut it into 6 inches circles. Place a dough circle on a lined up baking sheet. Place on the center of one side of it 2 tbsp of the filling.

5. Cover it with the other side of the dough circle and press its edges with a fork to seal them. Repeat the process with the remaining mix to make more stuffed pies. place them in the fridge for 1 h. Once the time is up, place a large skillet over medium heat. Heat about 1/4 inch of oil in it.

6. Add some of the pies to the hot oil and cook them until they become golden brown. Serve them with your favorite sauce. Enjoy..

Cajun Steak Roulade

Prep Time: 10 mins
Total Time: 1 hr 10 mins

Servings per Recipe: 8
Calories   33.9
Fat   1.5g
Cholesterol   9.1mg
Sodium   589.3mg
Carbohydrates   2.2g
Protein   2.8g

Ingredients

1 large round steak
1 lb lean ground meat
2 tsp salt
2 tsp red pepper flakes

1 C. finely diced onion
1 finely diced garlic clove

Directions

1. Before you do anything, preheat the oven to 375 F.
2. Season the steak with a 1 tsp of salt, and 1 tsp of red pepper flakes.
3. Get a large mixing bowl: Combine in it the meat with the remaining salt, red pepper flakes, onion and garlic. Mix them well.
4. Place the steak on a baking sheet. Spread over it the meat mix then roll it tightly. Use a kitchen twine to tie it.
5. Place the rolled steak in the middle of a piece of foil and wrap it around it. Place it in the oven and cook it for 1 h 35 min.
6. Once the time is up, discard the foil and bake the steak roulade for an extra 16 min. Serve it warm.
7. Enjoy.

ENJOY THE RECIPES?
KEEP ON COOKING
WITH 6 MORE FREE COOKBOOKS!

Visit our website and simply enter your email address to join the club and receive your 6 cookbooks.

http://booksumo.com/magnet

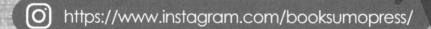
https://www.instagram.com/booksumopress/

https://www.facebook.com/booksumo/